Reconstruction: A Very Short Introduction

VERY SHORT INTRODUCTIONS are for anyone wanting a stimulating and accessible way into a new subject. They are written by experts, and have been translated into more than 45 different languages.

The series began in 1995, and now covers a wide variety of topics in every discipline. The VSI library currently contains over 550 volumes—a Very Short Introduction to everything from Psychology and Philosophy of Science to American History and Relativity—and continues to grow in every subject area.

Very Short Introductions available now:

Available soon:

For more information visit our web site

www.oup.com/vsi/

Allen C. Guelzo

RECONSTRUCTION

A Very Short Introduction

OXFORD
UNIVERSITY PRESS

OXFORD

UNIVERSITY PRESS

Oxford University Press is a department of the University of Oxford.
It furthers the University's objective of excellence in research, scholarship,
and education by publishing worldwide. Oxford is a registered trade mark of
Oxford University Press in the UK and certain other countries.

Published in the United States of America by Oxford University Press
198 Madison Avenue, New York, NY 10016, United States of America.

© Oxford University Press 2018, 2020

Published in hardcover as *Reconstruction: A Concise History* in 2018

Library of Congress Control Number: 2019948412

ISBN 978-0-19-045479-1

1 3 5 7 9 8 6 4 2

Printed in Great Britain
by Ashford Colour Press Ltd., Gosport, Hants.

Contents

Acknowledgments

Several talented and thoughtful historians and commentators took away time from their own schedules and their own more important tasks to read and review the manuscript of *Reconstruction*; I regret to admit that I have no better means of recognizing their generosity and perspicacity than these simple acknowledgments. James Oakes (City University of New York) was the first on whom I tried out the idea of Reconstruction as a bourgeois revolution, and his unfeigned interest fed the spark until it glowed. Louis Masur (Rutgers University) combed through each chapter, relentlessly sniffing out every gaffe and indiscretion, as did Jonathan White (Christopher Newport University). Michael Lind (New America Foundation), Steven Woodworth (Texas Christian University), Matthew Norman (University of Cincinnati), and Brian M. Jordan (Sam Houston State University) also volunteered themselves to read parts here and there. Any errors that might unfortunately appear in the interpretations and writing here must be blamed on me; however, any praise must be shared equally with all of those named above.

List of illustrations

Introduction

The era in US history known as Reconstruction forms a sort of coda to the traumatic years of the American Civil War, which lasted from 1861 to 1865. It embraces the twelve years of active effort to rebuild and reconstitute the American Union after the attempt by the Confederate States of America to secede from it, and in some sense (because it had no official starting or ending date) it spluttered on well into the 1890s.

But Reconstruction can also reasonably be characterized as the ugly duckling of American history. The twelve years that are the conventional designation of the Reconstruction period, from 1865 to 1877, teem with associations and developments that seem regrettable, if not simply baleful. They left a long legacy of bitterness, especially among Southerners who believed that they had fought an honorable war and were handed a dishonorable peace, as well as Southerners who refused to accept defeat and manufactured the myth of a glorious "Lost Cause" to justify themselves and their continuing belief in the rightness of the Confederate project. Reconstruction also coincided with an eruption of notorious levels of graft, corruption, and fraud in American civil governments—not least in the ones erected by federal force in the former rebel states. But Reconstruction is probably best known, and least liked, as the greatest missed opportunity Americans ever had to erase the treacherous impact of slavery and race in a reconstructed and unified nation. There is, in other words, something in Reconstruction for nearly every American to regret.

The term "reconstruction" actually surfaced even before the Civil War began in 1861, although in its first form it was a way of describing how the Constitution would have to be amended in order to accommodate the demands of the Southern states and head off their secession. "Sooner or later," predicted New York Democratic financier August Belmont, there must be "a national convention for the reconstruction of one government over all the States." The term resurfaced in 1862, this time to describe the pacification policies that the federal government might deploy once the Union armies had suppressed the Confederate rebellion. Articulating these policies turned out to be no easy matter. Abraham Lincoln, the president whose inauguration had triggered Southern secession in the first place, was never at ease using the word "reconstruction"—he qualified it with add-ons like "what is called reconstruction" or "a plan of reconstruction (as the phrase goes)"—and preferred to speak of the "re-inauguration of the national authority" or the need to "re-inaugurate loyal state governments."

But use it Lincoln did, however grudgingly, and he built all of his assumptions about the shape of Reconstruction on one single presupposition: the constitutional impossibility of secession. The Constitution granted no right to the states to secede; ergo, the Southern states had never really left the Union, and the so-called Confederate States were really only insurrectionary regimes. "I hold, that in contemplation of universal law, and of the Constitution, the Union of these States is perpetual," Lincoln said in his first inaugural address. On that basis, he sanctioned the creation of a Unionist Virginia government-in-exile and installed temporary "military governors" in areas of Tennessee, North Carolina, and Arkansas, who proposed to carry on the usual functions of state government as though secession (and the secessionists) had never existed.

But whatever the legal and constitutional arguments, the Confederacy did not look at all like a mere insurrection, like the Whiskey Rebellion or the Dorr Rebellion. It comprised eleven contiguous states, with a population of more than nine million (Belgium, by comparison, had a population of less than five million, Scandinavia eighteen million), and it created a new government larger than most European nation-states, along with armies to defend it. The "leaders of the South have made an army, and they have made what is more, they have made a nation," declared William Ewart Gladstone, the United Kingdom's chancellor of the exchequer.

Ironically, Gladstone's view was echoed by several of the most fervent members of Lincoln's own party, the Republicans. They had become known as "radicals" from the outset of the war, and though the term described only about half of the Senate's Republicans, and slightly more than that in the House of Representatives, they were unapologetic in asserting that the Confederate states had lost all title to statehood by seceding.

What had really happened when the Southern states seceded, Massachusetts senator Charles Sumner countered, was "State suicide or State forfeiture or State abdication." Whatever the name, secession had converted the old Southern states into something less than what they had been. What was more, it was the prerogative of Congress, not the president, to define that status and create the policies which control any ideas of reconstructing the Union. Thaddeus Stevens, Sumner's counterpart in the House of Representatives, wanted to go even further: "We propose to confiscate all the estates of every rebel belligerent whose estate was worth $10,000, or whose land exceeded two hundred acres in quantity." As for the Confederate leadership—and "how many captive enemies it would be proper to

3

execute, as an example to nations"—Stevens would bleakly "leave others to judge."

Lincoln, however, wanted no part of such a draconian reconstruction. For one thing, it was tantamount to conceding that the Confederates had been correct all along in claiming a right to withdraw from the Union. Lincoln laid out his first detailed strategy for "Amnesty and Reconstruction" in December 1863. He proposed to grant full pardons "with restoration of all rights of property, except as to slaves" to any inhabitants of Southern states reoccupied by federal military forces upon taking an oath of future loyalty (and keeping "said oath inviolate"). There were several categories of exceptions to this opportunity: "civil or diplomatic agents" of the Confederacy, military and naval officers, and those who had mistreated Union prisoners of war. But the purpose behind this apparent generosity was really political, because this strategy would grant Lincoln the authority to "re-establish a State government" as soon as the oath-takers numbered just 10 percent of the 1860 voting population in each state—while also ensuring that the "reinaugurated" state governments abolished slavery.

Many Republicans applauded Lincoln's plan as "glorious" and saw it as an enticement to Southerners not only to end the rebellion but to abandon slavery as well. "The President," wrote Ohio Republican James A. Garfield, "has struck a great blow for the country and himself." But so broad an offer infuriated Stevens and Sumner, who interpreted this approach to mean that traitors were being invited back into the Union with full privileges and with only one significant punishment, and by a president who meant to sideline Congress in overseeing the process. Opposition to Lincoln's plan within Congress (and within Lincoln's own party) was spearheaded by Ohio Senator Benjamin Wade and Maryland Congressman Henry Winter Davis, who designed a Reconstruction plan of their own: first, the required number of oath-takers was increased from 10 to 50 percent; then, a civilian provisional governor would be appointed, and the eligible voters would elect a state convention to write a new state constitution that would ban slavery and forbid rebel officers from serving in the legislature or as governor. Only then could these states resume their proper place in the Union and send representatives and senators to Congress. "Until majorities can be found loyal and trustworthy for state government," declared Wade, the South "must be governed by a stronger hand" than either Lincoln or its own repentant Unionists.

Lincoln scoffed at the Wade-Davis plan, and at the criticisms of his own plan, as tantamount to conceding that "states whenever they please may of their own motion dissolve their connection with the Union," the very constitutional issue that began the war. Moreover, Reconstruction was an executive branch responsibility, just as managing the war had been; Congress had nothing to do with it, any more than it had the authority to trespass on his military authority as commander in chief. (Lincoln said nothing about the role of the federal judiciary, which had been mostly silent during the war, but the judicial branch would soon seek to join the debate, too). So, although Lincoln protested that he was not "inflexibly committed to any single plan of restoration," he pocket-vetoed the Wade-Davis plan on July 8, 1864. Congressional Republicans made an effort to mollify Lincoln later that year when the House of Representatives' Committee on the Rebellious States (chaired by Henry Winter Davis) produced a Reconstruction bill that left open a shared role for the president and Congress in the process of Reconstruction. But in February 1865, opposition from uncooperative Democrats and unappeased Radical Republicans tabled it.

Not that Lincoln's own schemes for Reconstructing the Confederacy had shone with any success. When Union forces overran eastern North Carolina in the spring of 1862, Lincoln appointed Edward Stanly, a North Carolina Unionist, as "military governor" of North Carolina, and urged him to arrange the election of a Unionist member of Congress in the occupied zone. But Stanly could recruit only 864 voters for the election, and the House of Representatives refused to seat Stanly's candidate. Stanly was also at odds with Lincoln about the Emancipation Proclamation, and on January 15, 1863, Stanly resigned. Lincoln did not appoint a successor.

This inauspicious beginning was followed by another failure. Union forces recaptured more than half of Arkansas in 1862, and on July 19 of that year, Lincoln appointed John S. Phelps as military governor. A state constitutional convention met in Little Rock in January 1864 and elected Isaac Murphy as provisional governor. But the two senators and three congressmen they elected were also refused seats in Congress. The same pattern, with still more embarrassing developments, repeated itself in Louisiana. A military governor, George Shepley, was appointed by Lincoln for Louisiana after the US Navy captured New Orleans in April, 1862, and Lincoln urged him to organize congressional elections without waiting for a new state constitution.

The two congressman elected under Shepley's oversight on December 3, 1862, managed to persuade Congress to seat them. But after a Unionist state convention wrote a free-state constitution for Louisiana in 1864, the two senators elected by the Louisiana legislature were blocked from their seats by the Senate Judiciary Committee "till by some joint action of both Houses there shall be some recognition of an existing State government acting in harmony with the government of the United States." One of Lincoln's military governors, Andrew J. Hamilton, never even set foot in his home state of Texas. Only Andrew Johnson, the lone US senator from a seceding state to remain loyal to the Union, enjoyed any kind of success after Lincoln appointed him military governor of Tennessee, and even then, Johnson did not convene a new state constitutional convention until January 1865. This did not look much like the reconstruction of anything.

A second fundamental problem was the future status of the freed slaves. Not a single one of the haphazard experiments in Reconstruction conducted before the end of the war had specified what the future status of the freedpeople would be. Were they now supposed to sign contracts and be paid for their labor? Who would guarantee that the contracts would not turn out to be simply a newer version of bondage? Should provision be made out of the public purse to educate them? Should they be considered citizens, and entitled to all the "privileges and immunities" guaranteed to citizens by Article 4, section 2, of the Constitution? And what were those "privileges and immunities" anyway? Office-holding, jury service, bearing witness in court, voting, election to office?

One thing was politically certain: on the day slavery was abolished, the Constitutional rules on representation in the House of Representatives would undergo a complete change. The so-called three-fifths rule in the Constitution (which had prevented slaveholding states from counting more than three-fifths of their enslaved population as part of their total population in order to determine the number of representatives each slave state could send to Congress) would disappear, and going forward, every freed slave would be counted as a full person—yet without any right to vote. It was not beyond the realm of possibility that the defeated Southern states might send back to a postwar Congress, not only the same number of representatives they had been able to send before the eruption of war, but an additional thirteen representatives (by Thaddeus Stevens's reckoning) beyond what they had once elected. This unlooked-for increase in Southern representatives, if it was elected only by white Southern votes, would likely be composed entirely of old Southern Democrats who would find common cause with their old Northern Democratic allies. Together, they could put a swift end to the Republicans' wartime control of Congress and enable Congress to pass legislation repealing the Republicans' wartime domestic achievements (such as protective tariffs, government assistance to the railroads, the Homestead Act, and the national banking system), while burdening the US Treasury with the Confederacy's wartime debts. The idea of enfranchising the freed slaves would disappear entirely as a political possibility.

For that reason, Charles Sumner made a final desperate attempt to assert that "there can be no power under the Constitution to disenfranchise loyal people...especially when it may hand over the loyal majority to the government of the disloyal minority." Lincoln signaled that he understood this in his last speech, on April 11, 1865. He simultaneously chided Congress for refusing to admit the Louisiana senators, and urged the Louisiana Unionists to reconsider granting at least limited black voting rights by "extending the vote to the very intelligent, and...those who serve our cause as soldiers." They, at least, would be reliable safeguards for "the jewel of liberty." Beyond that, however, beckoned a future he described in Richmond on April 4 as one in which free black Americans "shall have all the rights which God has given to every other free citizen of this republic." As for the Confederates, he instinctively erred on the side of "malice toward none." He urged his generals to "let them have their horses to plow with, and, if you like, their guns to shoot crows with." He "wanted no one punished; treat them liberally all round," which he believed was the only way to get "those people to return to their allegiance to the Union and submit to the laws." Whatever else might have been contained in that strategy disappeared with Lincoln's assassination three days after his last speech.

One of the most-asked questions in American history must surely be, what would have happened in the Reconstruction era if Lincoln had lived? Lincoln was such a private person, and so tight-lipped a politician, that it is impossible to project what further plans he would have developed. And, if he had obeyed the unspoken two-term rule for occupying the presidency, he would only have been in office until March 1869, which is not a substantial period in which to effect something as momentous as Reconstruction. Nor were there any generally received models to guide Lincoln in such a process—or, indeed, anyone else throughout history who had faced a similar dilemma. The Roman civil wars divided on postwar policy, with Sulla crushing his surviving rivals with an iron fist, but with Pompey and Caesar opting for clemency and reconciliation. Henri IV brought an end to the strife of the sixteenth-century French Wars of Religion because he could advertise himself as an outsider, willing to conciliate all parties and eager to bring peace and prosperity to all. But across the English Channel, the restored monarchy of Charles II abandoned any notion of reconciliation, and hanged, drew, and quartered even the corpse of Oliver Cromwell, not to mention his living supporters. Closer in time to Reconstruction, the Taiping Rebellion in China was suppressed in 1864 in an orgy of massacres. Had Reconstruction been planned according to the Sulla, Stuart, or Taiping scripts, then proscription, trials, and executions might have continued for another generation.

But instead, American Reconstruction wears the garb of improvisation, uncertainty, and experiment—which historians have difficulty containing within narratives that thrive on direction, purpose, and determinism. The first non-participant historians of Reconstruction, James Ford Rhodes and William Archibald Dunning of Columbia University, bore down harshly on Reconstruction's missteps, largely because both were Democrats politically and had little sympathy for a Republican program. Although Rhodes and Dunning professed a kind of objective relativism, refusing to offer judgments on the faults or virtues of Reconstruction, the faults they found were usually with Republicans and the virtues Democratic. As a Progressive, Dunning (and those who followed in his train: Ulrich B. Phillips, J. G. Hamilton, Walter L. Fleming, Charles Ramsdell, and Merton Coulter) was suspicious of the follies and inefficiencies of democracy when spread too broadly. In his mind, Reconstruction brought not democracy to the South but mob rule and to Washington, nothing but vindictiveness and plunder.

Criticism of the Dunning School made its first appearance in the 1930s, beginning with the attacks launched at the Dunningites by William Edward Burghardt Du Bois in *Black Reconstruction* (1935) and James S. Allen in *Reconstruction: The Battle for Democracy* (1937). Reconstruction might not have been a proud achievement, but, Du Bois objected, Reconstruction led directly "to democratic government and the labor movement today." Allen agreed: "The destruction of the slave power was the basis for real national unity and the further development of capitalism, which would produce conditions most favorable for the growth of the labor movement."

Unhappily, neither Du Bois nor Allen possessed a broad platform from which to rally a countermovement, partly because of Du Bois's imperious self-isolation and Allen's identification with the Communist Party. It would not be until the 1960s, after the emergence of the civil rights movement as a "second Reconstruction," that the idols of the Dunning School began to fall. John Hope Franklin's *Reconstruction after the Civil War* (1961) and Kenneth Stampp's *The Era of Reconstruction, 1865–77* (1965) started the trend, to be followed by John and LaWanda Cox, George Bentley, Richard Current, Allen W. Trelease, Herman Belz, and finally by Eric Foner's massive *Reconstruction: America's Unfinished Revolution, 1863–1877* (1988).

Noble as their intentions were, the anti-Dunningites had their foibles, too. Du Bois and Allen were both writing from self-consciously Marxist frameworks that forbade any other understanding of Reconstruction but through class and revolution, with race sometimes deployed as a surrogate for class. "The emancipation of man is the emancipation of labor," Du Bois wrote, "and the emancipation of labor is the freeing of that basic majority of workers who are yellow, brown and black." Thus, Reconstruction should have been the moment when working-class blacks and whites together had an opportunity to create a new American economic and political order, only to have it yanked away by a nervous white Northern bourgeoisie who preferred making peace with the defeated Confederates to licensing a genuinely radical, biracial workers' movement.

Reconstruction was, in other words, seen as a typical bourgeois-democratic revolution, not unlike the initial phase of the French Revolution in 1789 or the liberal democratic revolutions across Europe in 1848. Like those uprisings, it pitted a capitalist, middle-class bourgeoisie over a slaveholding aristocracy, with the former striking up alliances with peasants on the land and workers in the tenements to overthrow the rule of the planter elite. This newly empowered bourgeoisie derived their authority, first, as the Southern Unionist allies of Union military victory, and second as the owners of capital and the possessors of professional and commercial income (rather than birthright or status). Alas, bourgeois revolutions frighten their own architects, who quickly come to see that in encouraging peasants and workers, they have created a Frankenstein monster that has no more respect for the bourgeoisie than it had for the aristocrats.

At that moment, "the bourgeoisie," wrote Lenin, "strives to put an end to the bourgeois revolution halfway from its destination, when freedom has been only half won, by a deal with the old authorities and the landlords." They strive "to reach a tacit pact with the old-landed aristocracy in order to preserve their power." But the genie cannot be stuffed back into the bottle; it is only stunned, and in time it will reawaken with renewed strength as the guide and leader of the socialist revolution, and finish off industrial capitalism, just as the bourgeoisie finished off the aristocrats. Du Bois in particular bears the impress of this notion of Reconstruction as a bourgeois revolution, for in Du Bois's telling, Reconstruction's "vision of democracy across racial lines" was undone by a "counterrevolution of property."

The principal difficulty with such a conventional Marxist narrative is that neither the Civil War nor Reconstruction fit neatly into it.

Both the Civil War and Reconstruction belong to a chapter in American history in which the United States was still an overwhelmingly agricultural economy, and the contest that was waged between 1861 and 1865 was largely an argument (in economic terms) between the free-labor family farm and the slave-labor cotton plantation.

Nor is there any evidence that the victorious Republicans who attempted to build a bourgeois South among the ruins of the old plantation order ever panicked at the prospect of empowering blacks or poor whites, or betrayed them by establishing a self-protecting alliance with the dethroned aristocrats. And the freedpeople hardly experienced a taste of Marxist alienation; they instead experienced bourgeois frustration at their exclusion from material accumulation and democratic and judicial process, and that was how they articulated it. If Reconstruction was indeed a bourgeois revolution, it was a *pure* bourgeois revolution—a self-contained revolutionary event outside the boundaries of Marxist theory. And if it failed, it was not because it sold out, but because it was overthrown by the resurgent political power of a bloodied but unbowed aristocracy.

It was also easy, in the midst of so many shortcomings and failures in Reconstruction, for the anti-Dunningites to overlook four important ways in which Reconstruction actually succeeded:

- Reconstruction restored a federal Union, for which the North had been fighting from the start, and corrected the centrifugal forces of the American federal Union that had brought on the war in the first place.

- Reconstruction followed the route of generosity—it created no conquered provinces, no mass executions for treason. As Walt Whitman wrote, almost in self-congratulation, Reconstruction "has been paralleled nowhere in the world—in any other country on the globe the whole batch of the Confederate leaders would have had their heads cut off." Ironically, most of the violence that pockmarked Reconstruction was inflicted on the victors, not the vanquished.

- The freedpeople made only modest economic gains in moving out of the shadow of slavery into freedom and self-ownership. But there were still beachheads for black Southerners all across the South in terms of property ownership and embourgeoisment, which would form the soil out of which the civil rights movement would flourish eighty years later.

- In the same fashion, Reconstruction established, beyond a doubt, the legal equality of all Americans under the banner of citizenship. Much of that equality was compromised by racial prejudice, vigilante violence, and the twisting of law. But it was not extinguished, and the Reconstruction-era amendments to the Constitution (the Thirteenth, Fourteenth, and Fifteenth) have together formed the last on which injustice, racial prejudice, and inequality have repeatedly been hammered down.

Not everything that should have been gained was gained in Reconstruction; but not everything was lost, either.

Historical writing on Reconstruction has expanded exponentially since the 1960s, pushing the boundaries of Reconstruction historiography into new subfields of time, labor, geography, gender, family, and economics. The American West has increasingly become part of the Reconstruction schema, starting with the military subjugation of the Plains Indian tribes, but increasingly reaching to include the challenge posed to an American Protestant culture by the Mormon colony of Utah and the racial triangle formed by Cherokee slavery and segregation. There is now a greater sense of the continuity of Reconstruction backward to the war years (as in, for example, connecting the activities of Civil War guerrillas with the postwar insurgency of the Ku Klux Klan) and forward to the civil rights movement of the 1960s. Studies of the experience of veterans, both Northern and

Southern, in Reconstruction have only just begun to come to the fore, as have also inquiries into how, with a certain postmodern twist, Reconstruction influenced the memory of the Civil War and, in addition, generated its own historical memory. Even the conventional chronology of Reconstruction has been reworked, so that in some cases the starting point has been pushed back well into the Civil War years, and in others substantially far forward, to the beginning of Jim Crow segregation in the 1890s. For the purposes here, it will be easiest if Reconstruction is thought of as four discrete movements:

- Early Reconstruction, from the first of Lincoln's experiments in 1862 until the announcement of Andrew Johnson's appointment of provisional governors for the Southern states in 1865;

- Presidential (or executive) Reconstruction, covering the short-lived Johnson governments, from mid-1865 to the passage of the Congressional Reconstruction Acts in 1867, which attempted to curtail the liberties of the freed slaves and return ex-Confederates to Washington as members of Congress;

- Congressional Reconstruction, which begins with the Reconstruction Acts and concludes with the readmission, under the terms of those statutes, of the last of the one-time Confederate states to representation in Congress in 1870, during which time the Fourteenth and Fifteenth Amendments to the Constitution empowered the emergence of a black political leadership class; and

- Overthrow of Reconstruction, from 1870, when the first white Democratic regimes were elected to "redeem" the southern states from Republican control, until 1877, when the last Southern Republican governments, in South Carolina and Louisiana, were extinguished.

One may also speak of an "Aftermath" of Reconstruction, from 1877 until 1896, to include the increasingly oppressive nature of the "Redeemer" regimes, the capture of both houses of Congress and the executive branch by Democrats in 1893, and the disastrous decision in the case of *Plessy v. Ferguson* to give federal countenance to racial segregation. Some of these categories are porous: Virginia, for instance, was readmitted under the Reconstruction Acts in 1870, but had already returned the Democratic party to effective power four months before, only to witness the rise of a "Readjuster" movement in the 1880s which fused black Republicans and moderate Democrats; and Tennessee was never included in the Reconstruction Acts and was readmitted to Congress in 1866. But they will serve as a general timeline.

Awareness of the increasing varieties of Reconstruction interpretation will not prevent *Reconstruction: A Concise History* from committing some offenses, mostly in the interest of remaining short. Extensive explorations of gender, family, veterans, philosophy, literature—all of them, unhappily, are beyond the scope of a series whose volumes, to be fair, are intended to each offer but a brief introduction to the topic at hand. This small offering will attempt no more than to fashion a basic scaffolding for understanding Reconstruction, leaving the vaster structures of elaboration and interpretation to improvised *ad libitum*.

Chapter 1
Vengeance: April–December 1865

"Today the city is wild with grief and anger over the report that President Lincoln was assassinated last night by a Southerner, John Wilkes Booth," wrote a newly discharged Union lieutenant in Lowell, Massachusetts, on April 15, 1865. "All flags are at half-mast, public and private buildings draped in black, and business is suspended.... It is all a man's life is worth to show any feeling but sorrow or anger." The scene in Lowell was repeated across the North that day. In Philadelphia, "old men bowed their heads in sorrow and wept like children." On every block of Chestnut Street, between Third and Thirteenth, "the whole street, as far as the eye could stretch, was wailing the loss of the Chief Magistrate of the nation." And not the least in mourning was Washington, DC, where only a few hours were allowed to elapse in the capital before Lincoln's vice president, Andrew Johnson, was sworn in as the seventeenth president by Chief Justice Salmon P. Chase.

Johnson had not been an obvious choice as Lincoln's vice president. When Lincoln was elected president in 1860, his vice president was Hannibal Hamlin, a Maine abolitionist who had left the Democratic Party for the Republicans. But Hamlin had not been a consequential figure, and in 1864 the Republican National Convention substituted Johnson, a lifelong Tennessee Democrat, on Lincoln's reelection ticket as a way of demonstrating the Republicans' bipartisan dedication to re-union. Although Johnson never openly embraced the Republicans, he had earned warm applause in the North for his lonely refusal, at the beginning of the war, to abandon his seat in the US Senate and follow Tennessee into secession. He also had the advantage of having been reasonably successful as Lincoln's military governor of Tennessee from 1862 to 1865, and he had commended himself to the most radical members of Lincoln's Republican Party for promising black Tennesseans in October 1864 that he would be "your Moses, and lead you through the Red Sea of war and bondage to a fairer future of liberty and peace."

At the same time, Johnson was also a loner, an outsider in Washington politics who concealed his insecurities behind a wall of quiet. Lincoln was taken aback when Johnson suggested that political business in Tennessee should excuse him from attending his own inauguration, and he nearly sank himself into political oblivion when he did show up for the inauguration, visibly intoxicated, and proceeded to deliver a rambling monologue that sent eyes rolling helplessly upward. "This Johnson is a queer man," Lincoln remarked, and in April, when Lincoln visited Richmond, he ignored a suggestion that he and Johnson meet in the ruined ashes of the Confederate capital.

Any uncertainties Johnson generated, though, were banished in the wake of Lincoln's assassination by Johnson's promises to deal harshly with the guilty Confederacy. Indeed, it was not only Lincoln's death that motivated Johnson; John Langdon Sibley, the librarian of Harvard College, was deeply depressed to see the swelling numbers of "infirm men & cripples in the streets.... The terrible battles which have been fought have been turning out more & more, & it is painful to see the large number...who have lost an arm or a leg or are otherwise maimed & move on crutches." When the members of Congress's Joint Committee on the Conduct of the War called on Johnson the day after Lincoln's death, he assured them that he would deal harshly with the rebels who had been responsible for the war and the assassination. "Robbery is a crime; rape is a crime; murder is a crime; *treason* is a crime, and *crime* must be punished." The perpetrators of those crimes included many more than just John Wilkes Booth (who was still at large). Johnson continued, "Treason must be made infamous and traitors must be impoverished." Radical Republicans were delighted: the Confederacy, wrote Michigan senator Jacob Howard, "should be made to bear the brand of dishonor & enduring shame."

How this sentiment was to be translated into policy was another question, however. Reconstruction of the Union would require dealing with a thorny hedge of legal, constitutional, and political questions. Were the eleven states that seceded to form the Confederacy in 1861 still states in any meaningful sense of the term? Radical Republicans certainly thought not, and now that Lincoln was no more, the way seemed clear for Congress to step forward and reshape the South in the same way the Constitution authorized Congress to oversee the federal territories in the West. And what was the standing of the Confederacy's ordinary legal actions? Was the federal government obligated to assume the debts that the Confederate states had contracted during the war? Above all, what was to become of the 3.9 million emancipated African Americans whose legal status as chattel had been extinguished by the war, by Lincoln's Emancipation Proclamation, and by the Thirteenth Amendment? "Shall they be men; be clothed with the rights and duties of freemen," asked the Union League of Philadelphia, "or shall they be returned to a worse slavery than that from which we have freed them? . . . Shall our old notions about race and color shut our eyes to the manifest march of the times or shall we accept and solve the problem with truth and reason?"

For the moment, Andrew Johnson had to concentrate his attention on ending the war. The rebel army surrendered by Robert E. Lee, and the paroled by General Ulysses S. Grant, at Appomattox Court House on April 9, 1865, was the most

1. In 1865, Andrew Johnson was described by the newspaper editor Alexander K. McClure as "about five feet ten in height, rather stoutly and symmetrically built, . . . rather a cold grey eye that looks as if in its calmest glances there slumbers behind it quite enough to quicken it; a finely chiseled Roman face, usually sad in expression, at time relieved by a genial smile, and in manner and dress serenely plain and unaffected."

important, but not the only, Confederate army still in existence. Negotiations were already under way for the surrender of the next-largest Confederate force, in North Carolina. Meanwhile, the assassin Booth dodged federal pursuers until he was cornered in a tobacco barn in Virginia on April 26 and shot to death, and Confederate president Jefferson Davis and his cabinet would remain beyond federal reach until Union cavalry captured them near Irwinville, Georgia, on May 10. Two other Confederate commands in Alabama and Texas would not surrender until May 4 and May 26.

Unlike the rebel parolees at Appomattox, few of these other defeated Confederates had much hope for mercy, especially from Andrew Johnson. The new president had already authorized the trial of John Wilkes Booth's collaborators in a military tribunal rather than in a civil court, and the only question seemed to be how many of them would be hanged. When Union general William T. Sherman appeared to have granted excessively lenient terms to the Confederate army in North Carolina that included "recognition" of the wartime Confederate state governments and the "practical" cancellation of "the confiscation laws, and relieved rebels of every degree…from all pains and penalties for their crimes," Sherman was swiftly rebuked and ordered to renegotiate the surrender. It was "clear and settled" in Johnson's mind "that no civil authority should be recognized which has its source in rebel election or appointment." This gave Johnson all the appearance of an avenging angel, and even hesitant Northerners suspected that "the presidential chair is occupied by a man who has pledged himself to make the blood of the educated and influential rebels run in streams."

But despite his newfound radical reputation, Johnson's bark was very different from his bite. Lincoln and the leadership of the Republican radicals had been Whigs (before 1856, when the Whig Party collapsed over the slavery issue); Johnson was, as one English observer shrewdly perceived, "a Democrat…of the [Andrew] Jackson type" who believed "that freedom in the United States ought to tend toward social equality"—although the equality Jacksonians had in mind did not extend across the divide of race. He "had a latent hostility towards money-power, and the aggregation of property, as essentially aristocratic." But he had owned slaves himself and (as Indiana congressman George W. Julian discovered) "was, at heart, as decided a hater of the negro and of everything savoring of abolitionism, as the rebels from whom he had separated." His real animus was directed at the plantation nabobs, and he extended his grudge against the planter class to Northern financiers. "The aristocracy based on negro property disappears at the Southern end of the line," he snarled, "but only to reappear in an oligarchy of bonds and national securities in the States which suppressed the rebellion." Although he did not mind promising to be the freedmen's Moses, he did not expect the Promised Land to make them the social or political equals of whites. "I am for a *white* Mans [*sic*] Government in America," he told a Tennessee supporter.

Gradually, Johnson began rolling back the wartime measures Lincoln had improvised from 1861 onward. At first, these rollbacks were uncontroversial: on April 29, he lifted the sanctions on trade with the former Confederate states east of the Mississippi; on May 9, he formally recognized the Virginia government-in-exile (which had been established in 1862 under Francis Pierpont) as the new Virginia state government; and on May 22, he formally dissolved the US Navy's blockade of Confederate ports. He gave particular cheer to Radical Republican hearts on May 15, when he appointed the "Christian soldier," the unapologetically evangelical Major General Oliver Otis Howard, to head the newly created Bureau of Refugees, Freedmen and Abandoned Lands (which became known simply as the Freedmen's Bureau) and begin redistributing to the freedpeople "all the abandoned lands, and those in the Government's possession under the Confiscation Act, and all those acquired by Treasury tax sales or otherwise."

The cheer began to dissipate, however, on May 29, when Johnson issued a proclamation, built on Lincoln's December 1863 amnesty proclamation, granting "to all persons who have, directly or indirectly, participated in the existing rebellion.... amnesty and pardon, with restoration of all rights and property, except as to slaves and except in cases where legal proceedings under the laws of the United States providing for the confiscation of property...have been instituted." There followed a long list of exclusions—"civil or diplomatic officers" of the Confederacy, "military or naval officers...above the rank of colonel in the army or lieutenant in the navy," and any Southerners "who have voluntarily participated in said rebellion…whose taxable property is over $20,000." But even the most notorious could still make "special application" to Johnson for executive clemency.

The intent of the proclamation puzzled congressional Republicans. "It was supposed that President Johnson would err, if at all, in imposing too harsh terms" on the rebels, recalled Ohio US senator John Sherman. After all, Johnson himself repeatedly claimed that he wanted "the prompt initiation of legal proceedings against the leaders of the civil war." But as it turned out, what he really wanted was for them to come to him on bended knee and experience some of the humiliation he had lived with as a "plebian." After that, he was more than satisfied to trade the garb of Moses for that of Pharoah. When John Eaton, who had been the general commissioner of freedmen in Tennessee, pressed Johnson about "establishing schools and organizing new industries" for the freedmen, Johnson's habitual curtain of silence descended. "He was quite obviously bored, and all that might have been said on the subject had no more inclination to stay by him than has water to stay on a duck's back."

Puzzlement turned to anger with the release of a second presidential proclamation, this time authorizing the appointment of a civilian "provisional governor" for North Carolina. The person chosen for this new position was William W. Holden, who had voted in favor of secession in 1861 but then transformed himself into a "peace" candidate for governor of North Carolina in 1864. Holden was charged with "convening a convention…for the purpose of altering or amending" the state constitution and "to restore said State to its constitutional relations to the Federal government." In short order, through June and July, Johnson proceeded to do likewise for Mississippi (where he appointed as governor William L. Sharkey, "a man of mind and culture," a judge and former Whig, but "offensive…on the subject of slavery"), Georgia (where he installed James Johnson, a Unionist lawyer and personal friend from Johnson's days in Congress, in the governorship), Texas (where Andrew Hamilton, who had fumbled Lincoln's appointment as a military governor of Texas, now became provisional civilian governor), Alabama (Lewis Parsons, a New York–born lawyer who had briefly held a Confederate army commission), South Carolina (Benjamin F. Perry, a Unionist newspaper editor who had also agreed to serve as a Confederate judge), and finally Florida (here the nominee was William Marvin, a former federal district judge who had actually spent most of the war practicing law in New York City).

It took some convincing to believe that these nominees were the best men to reestablish the vacant courts and the wrecked machinery of day-to-day governance, to summon state conventions, and to encourage the conventions to erase all traces of slavery from the state statute books. "For Gods [*sic*] Sake appoint a Sober man," erupted a fellow Tennessee Unionist, "instead of A.J. Hamilton; better known as drunken Jack Hamilton." What was more appalling was the realization that Johnson's governors promised to do little more than return the South, and the freed slaves, to a status only marginally different from what had prevailed before the war. These "quondam rebels," complained a Louisianan who had suffered real "rebel persecution," may "talk like union men and have ears like union men but they don't smell much like union men."

What incensed Republicans in particular was that Johnson set up civilian governments without so much as a by-your-leave to Congress, which had closed the last session of the Thirty-Eighth Congress on March 3, 1865 (the Senate stayed in special session until March 14) and would not reconvene as the new Thirty-Ninth Congress until December. It was one thing to create military governors, since their authority came strictly from Johnson's constitutional position as commander in chief of the army and navy and would expire the moment Johnson declared the war emergency over. But appointing *civilian* governors was a gesture ominously similar to Congress's authority to appoint civilian governors for the territories, and it implied that Johnson was reaching for much more power than Lincoln had ever dreamt or that Congress was willing to relinquish. "How the executive can remoddle [sic] the *States in the union* is past my comprehension," roared Thaddeus Stevens. He could see "how he could govern them through military governors until they are recognized," but civilian governments were "a question for the Legislative power exclusively." But worse still were the omissions in Johnson's proclamations: not a word about the Confederate and state war debts, nor any eligibility restrictions on ex-Confederates who had received amnesty or who would receive it after applying to Johnson, nor the slightest indication that the state constitutional conventions were obliged to consider the civil rights—and especially voting rights—of the freedmen.

The émigré Republican Carl Schurz, who had spent most of the war as a Union general, chided Johnson for proclamations that have "been generally interpreted as a declaration of policy on your part adverse to the introduction of negro suffrage....The old pro-slavery and disloyal element, I mean the oath-taking rebels," he predicted, would seize control. To Charles Sumner, it seemed pure political apostasy. "Andrew Johnson is the impersonation of the tyrannical slave power. In him it lives again." But Johnson waved the protests away. He had never stopped considering himself a Southerner and "cherished the kindest feeling towards the people of the Southern States." He told a South Carolina delegation that Reconstruction was really a "question of restoration," and he expected that the procedures described in his proclamations would so accelerate that process that the entire work of Reconstruction might be finished by the time Congress reconvened.

To recalcitrant Southerners, the proclamations were like a second wind. In the weeks after Appomattox, Hannah Rawlins (of Orange County, Virginia) confessed to feeling "as if it could not be reality, but...some hideous nightmare" that the Confederacy was no more. Stunned into passivity by the surrender, Rawlins remembered that "for three days after we learned of the fate of our devoted army, I don't think there were a dozen sentences spoken in the family where I was. A stranger would have thought there was a corpse in the house." But the passivity was only temporary and not the same thing as acquiescence. The war had pushed many Southerners beyond the point of reconciliation to their conquerors. "A lady near by," recorded Confederate War Department clerk J. B. Jones, "while surveying her dilapidated shoes, and the tattered sleeping gowns of her children, burst forth... 'I pray that I may live to see the United States involved in a war with some foreign power, which will make refugees of her people, and lay her cities in ashes!' " One Virginia woman believed that "the feeling here against the North is intense, tho' smothered.... Mothers will teach their young children to abhor the slayers of their fathers and brothers, they will teach it to them from their earliest infancy. Had I sons, this is the religion that I would inculcate from the time they could lisp." The Johnson proclamations revived Southern hopes for pulling some form of victory back from the abyss of defeat and seemed to the Cincinnati journalist Whitelaw Reid "to have called into active utterance all the hostility to Northerners." Strategies of resistance now began to take substance, and Confederate veteran Reuban Wilson hoped that "with the aid of the democratic party (which is bound to be very strong) of the north we will be able to check the republican party in their wild scheme."

Meanwhile, Johnson unwittingly fed the tidal return of Southern defiance. Petitions for pardons came in by the hundreds, and were given the presidential signature by the hundreds, from General George Pickett (of "Pickett's Charge" fame at Gettysburg) and Alexander H. Stephens (the Confederate vice president) to James A. Cheatham, a Confederate postmaster and railroad station agent. Ultimately, Johnson would issue 13,500 pardons by the fall of 1867 and had to appoint a pardon clerk, Matthew Pleasants, just to deal with the correspondence.

Once Johnson's provisional governors had arranged for the election of their state conventions, Republican confidence turned to disbelieving fury, as offices and legislatures filled up with generously pardoned Confederates, who only a few months before had been striving to overturn the government they now expected to rejoin. William Holden called for the election of North Carolina's state convention on September 21, but when it assembled on October 2 in Raleigh, it was top-heavy with ex-Confederate officers: Dennis D. Ferebee, the colonel of the Fifty-Ninth North Carolina; Samuel H. Walkup, lieutenant colonel of the Forty-Eighth North Carolina; Giles Mebane, a member of the 1861 secession convention and speaker of the North Carolina state senate. Almost their first concerns were "the State's assuming the debt contracted during the rebellion" (as though North Carolina's Confederate expenses were as legal as any other debt) and granting immunity from prosecution to any "person who have aided in the passage or execution of any law of the State of North-Carolina or of the Confederate States." This pattern was repeated in Mississippi's convention in August, over the protest of "the colored citizens of Mississippi" who feared "that the Legislature will pass such proscriptive laws as will drive the freedmen from the State, or practically re-enslave them."

Nothing, however, offered more calculated defiance than the representatives and senators whom the newly revived Southern states proposed to send to the opening of the Thirty-Ninth Congress. The new Georgia legislature defied reason by dispatching as Georgia's two senators the former Confederate vice president, Alexander Stephens, and former Confederate senator Herschel V. Johnson; South Carolinians elected to the House of Representatives a Confederate general, Samuel McGowan, as did Alabama, which elected Cullen A. Battle. All told, Johnson's self-reconstructed states chose for senators and representatives (in addition to Stephens) six Confederate cabinet officers, four Confederate generals, and fifty-eight members of the Confederate Congress.

Throughout all of these deliberations, not a single one of the rehabilitated legislatures took any step in favor of civil rights for the freedpeople. To the contrary, the new state legislature created by the Alabama state convention ratified the Thirteenth Amendment with the express reservation that "it does not confer upon Congress the power to legislate upon the political status of freedmen in this State." Even worse, freshly elected state legislatures in six states created a hedge of "black codes," designed to bind the freedmen into, for all practical purposes, peonage. Beginning in the Mississippi legislature on November 22, the "black codes" defined as "vagrants" or "paupers" any freedperson who appeared unemployed, and allowed local officials to bid them out (as they had once been at slave auctions) as laborers for up to a year. Other provisions of the codes forbade black-white intermarriage; curtailed free speech (including "insulting gestures"); and most ominous of all, banned freepeople from owning firearms, ammunition, and even knives.

This was not what Johnson had been expecting. He warned the provisional governors to mind their states' behavior, given that Congress would have the ultimate word on their future, and he even pressed his governor in Mississippi, William Sharkey, to "extend the elective franchise to all persons of color who can read the Constitution of the United States in English and write their names, and to all persons of color who own real estate valued at not less than two hundred and fifty dollars, and pay taxes thereon." In November, he tried to make it clear to Alexander Stephens that showing up for the next session of Congress as though he was only suffering from four years' worth of amnesia would be "exceedingly impolitic." Above all, Johnson did not withdraw federal troops from the South. Although the Union armies began demobilizing at rapid rates, there were still ninety thousand soldiers in uniform at the end of the year, spread over three hundred posts across the former Confederacy, and exercising a dual jurisdiction with Johnson's self-reconstructed governments.

These cautions garnered Johnson no sympathy whatsoever from the Republicans, whose disenchantment with the president rose hand in hand with their incredulity at the actions of new Southern state governments. "We almost believed him honest," charged the abolitionist and feminist journalist Jane Grey Swisshelm, but "we now fall back upon first impressions":

> The first time we saw him was at the great Union meeting in the Capitol, in April 1863. His speech then was like all his succeeding speeches, all about Andrew Johnson, and him crucified, and every idea three times expressed. We greatly regretted his nomination, but friends persuaded us, almost, that we were mistaken, and we made our second effort at playing conservative by coddling poor Andy Johnson by way of aiding thousands of honest men in their vain efforts to troll him along the path of rectitude, as sheep are led by walking before with a pan of salt.

Party conventions in Massachusetts and Ohio that summer saw barely restrained outbreaks of protest against the Johnson governments. By July, Charles Sumner was suspected by Navy Secretary Gideon Welles of "organizing and drilling...to make war upon the Administration policy and the Administration itself." Ohio's Benjamin Wade worried about the practical effect of Johnson's decisions on the Republican Party itself. "To admit the States on Mr. Johnson's plan," Wade confided to Sumner, would compromise the party's control of Congress and amount to "nothing less than political suicide."

Remembering the unhappy result of the Wade-Davis reconstruction plan, Ben Wade was not eager to engage in another political war with a president. Johnson, after all, had control of the vast web of executive patronage, and Wade feared that "too many men…wanted their brothers and friends appointed to office, and knew that Andy was bidding high for votes." But when Wade called on Johnson at the White House, he found the president's "ante-room full of rebels and Copperheads," and Wade soon concluded that Johnson intended to "subordinate…Congress and the Judiciary" to the "Executive."

Matters came to a head two days before the opening of Congress, as newly arrived congressional Republicans in Washington caucused in the Capitol. Thaddeus Stevens, who was convinced that "we must put the rebel states under territorial governments at once," called for the creation of a joint House-Senate committee of fifteen members, modeled on the wartime Joint Committee on the Conduct of the War, to determine whether the Johnson-appointed state governments were sufficiently sanitized of rebellion to merit the readmission of their representatives to Congress. The joint committee's report would decide the standing, not only of Johnson's rehabilitated states, but also Tennessee (which had reinstituted a civilian government in February 1865, and then elected eight congressmen in July), Louisiana, and Francis Pierpont's Virginia. Until such a report was submitted, "no member shall be received into either House from any of the so-called Confederate States." But lurking at the back of Radical minds was a bigger question: would the political confrontation that was brewing tip the country back into a fresh civil war? That would very much depend on what happened on the day the new Congress assembled.

Chapter 2

Alienation: December 1865– March 1867

The Radical Republicans arrived in Washington for the opening of Congress on December 4, 1865, with two major weapons at their disposal. One was the party caucus, especially in the Senate, where, Minnesota senator Morton Wilkinson reported, "Republican Senators used to meet almost every day...so as to leave no chance for hesitation, or division." The other was the lopsided majorities Republicans had won on Lincoln's coattails in both the House and Senate—37 out of 48 seats in the Senate, 132 out of 191 in the House—both of them sufficient to override presidential vetoes. The caucus moved to protect those majorities by the simple device of instructing the clerk of the House of Representatives, Edward McPherson, to "omit the names of the Representatives elect from all of the States heretofore declared in insurrection" from the initial roll call of the House "and close the doors of Congress to this rebel invasion." As McPherson called the truncated roll, Thaddeus Stevens was ready with the caucus's resolution to create a joint committee "for the purpose of considering the condition of the so-called Confederate States of America." It was adopted by an outsize 129 to 35 vote.

Johnson was not unaware of what Stevens and the caucus had been plotting. Nevertheless, he was still obliged to act as the head of the coalition that had dominated the wartime Congresses, and he hoped to defuse Radical wrath through the annual presidential message to Congress the next day. No one, he argued, should think that the solution to Reconstruction was to manage it from the Capitol. If "it is not one of the rights of any State government to renounce its own place in the Union," then Congress does not have the right to demote them to territorial status or exclude their representatives from the US government. He also struggled to shut down the possibility of granting voting rights to the freed slaves. The federal government had no more constitutional power to require the enfranchising of Southern freedpeople than it had to enfranchise free blacks "in the Northern, Middle, and Western States"—and he knew very well that three states (Connecticut, Wisconsin, and Minnesota) had just voted such measures down, and that Congress knew it, too.

This was not an unreasonable appeal, and Johnson sought to add to it some of his favorite distractions—"monopolies, perpetuities, and class legislation," and a Jacksonian "return to the standard of gold and silver"—to make it appear even more reasonable. He was wasting his words. A Republican juggernaut was already in motion that would produce, over the next seven months, a flurry of legislation, speeches, and reports designed to dissolve the self-reconstructed governments, extend voting rights to the freedmen by national authority, and reach past Johnson's hands to seize the reins of Reconstruction for Congress.

The first gestures were the easiest. The formation of a Joint Committee on Reconstruction was rolled through the House on the first day of the session. On December 5, 1865, William D. Kelley (a wartime Democrat-turned-Republican who was known as "Pig-Iron Kelley" for his efforts to shield Pennsylvania coal behind import tariffs) introduced a bill to legalize black voting rights in the District of Columbia—one jurisdiction where there was no question about Congress's direct authority to legislate. When the roll was called on it five and a half weeks later, the District voting bill sailed through, 116 to 54, and, as the *Chicago Tribune* reported, was "greeted in the galleries and on the floor with loud demonstrations of applause, which the Speaker [of the House, Schuyler Colfax] was for some time unable to check."

Then, on December 19, Lyman Trumbull introduced a bill in the Senate to extend the life of the Freedmen's Bureau beyond its original one-year authorization, giving it new support from the War Department and new responsibilities as the "guardian" of the freedpeople; it would arbitrate disputes; oversee the establishment of schools; "set apart for the use of freedmen…unoccupied public lands in Florida, Mississippi, Alabama, Louisiana, and Arkansas"; and subdivide land seized under the wartime Confiscation Acts into "parcels not exceeding forty acres" for "the loyal refugees and freedmen." It, too, easily passed in the Senate on January 25, and in the House, on February 6, by a luxuriously comfortable margin of 136 to 33.

A fourth proposal dealt directly with the nationalization of civil rights. Lyman Trumbull once more stepped forward as a legislative ghostwriter, introducing "An Act to protect all Persons in the United States in their Civil Rights, and furnish the Means of their Vindication" on January 5, 1866. The bill opened by affirming that

> all persons born in the United States and not subject to any foreign power, excluding Indians not taxed, are hereby declared to be citizens of the United States; and such citizens, of every race and color, without regard to any previous condition of slavery or involuntary servitude…shall have the same right, in every State and Territory in the United States, to make and enforce contracts, to sue, be parties, and give evidence, inherit, purchase, lease, sell, hold, and convey real and personal property, and to full and equal benefit of all laws and proceedings for the security of person and property.

Part of this bill faced backward, to the US Supreme Court's decision in the Dred Scott case of 1857. *Dred Scott v. Sanford* denied that blacks, slave or free, could ever qualify as citizens, or enjoy any of the Constitution's other "privileges and immunities." Curiously, the Constitution had never defined citizenship, either at the federal or state level. But this oversight only allowed Chief Justice Roger B. Taney, the author of the *Dred Scott* decision, to insert his own definition, on the basis of *jus sanguinis*—that is, citizenship by specific birthright. The birthright Taney had in mind was whiteness, and he used it to deny citizenship to anyone of "African descent." But in 1866, Taney was dead and gone, and Trumbull's civil rights bill aimed to bury Dred Scott with him by defining US citizenship by the rule of *jus soli*—or, by birth on US soil.

Neither the new joint committee nor Trumbull's civil rights bill was designed to make Andrew Johnson happy, and Navy Secretary Welles heard him express "himself…with sharpness" in a cabinet meeting about "the manner in which things had been got up by the Radicals before the session." But on the other hand, none of these bills exactly offered him a direct challenge. Trumbull had gone out of his way to mollify Johnson on the civil rights bill. Private interviews with Johnson had given Trumbull "just expectations" that the civil rights bill would satisfy the president, especially because Trumbull had cautiously avoided any reference to the act of voting itself as a "protected" right. When the Senate approved the bill on February 2, by a 33 to 12 vote, Trumbull had every reason to assume "that the President's aims, like his own, were in the direction of peace and concord."

It was not the first time a politician had mistaken Andrew Johnson's moody silences for assent. The critics of Johnson's self-reconstruction regimes had lit a slow-burning fire inside of him, and the activities of the Freedmen's Bureau only fanned it. Disturbed by the "small, endless, mean little injustice of every day" for the freedpeople, Otis Howard created a system of bureau courts to handle magistrate-level cases—and thereby take them out of the hands of Southern civil courts. In July, Howard issued a circular to his assistant commissioners in the bureau in July, authorizing them "to select...such confiscated and abandoned property as they deemed necessary" and designate it "for the immediate use for the life and comfort of refugees and freedmen." Johnson saw that this would collide with his amnesty proclamation, and abruptly ordered Howard "to return all abandoned lands to owners who were pardoned by the President, and provided no indemnity whatever for the occupants, refugees, or freedmen."

Johnson expected Congress to take the hints he had so helpfully sprinkled through his annual message in December and curtail Howard's activities. When it did not, he followed those hints on December 18 with a second message, laying out a little more impatiently how his measures were the best strategy to persuade the restored states "to confer upon the freedmen the privileges which are essential of their comfort, protection, and security." He finally applied the torch on February 19, by issuing a veto of the Freedmen's Bureau Bill and following that a month later with a veto of Trumbull's civil rights bill. And when the District of Columbia voting rights bill finally emerged from the Senate later in the year, Johnson vetoed that, too.

The veto of the Freedmen's Bureau Bill touched off an uproar in Congress. Johnson, complained the *Chicago Tribune*, had yielded to "the whisperings of the tempting copperhead serpent, and...treacherously stabbed to the heart this measure of benevolence." Nevertheless, some Republicans in the Senate now wavered, rather than force an outright split with the president. Painfully, an attempt to override Johnson's veto fell two votes short of the necessary two-thirds majority.

These divisions emboldened Johnson: on April 2, he issued yet another presidential order, declaring that "there now exists no organized armed resistance...to the authority of the United States." The wartime powers which had justified "military

2. A modern mural in the Capitol rotunda portrays the passage of the Civil Rights Bill in 1866. In the foreground, Henry Highland Garnet, who had been born a slave in Maryland, speaks with newspaper editor Horace Greeley, who supported African American suffrage. The vote was greeted with applause and cheering that lasted several minutes.

occupation, martial law, military tribunals, and the suspension of the privilege of the writ of habeas corpus" evaporated at a click of the telegraph key. The new Southern governors would no longer have to cope with suspicious department commandants, and the Freedmen's Bureau would lose any enforcement power over the freedmen's land claims and working conditions.

Congress usually avoided butting heads with a president of its own party; John Tyler had done likewise when he, like Johnson, inherited the presidency in 1841 from the deceased William Henry Harrison. But on this occasion, Johnson was listening to voices that prophesied that "another civil war is pending and that the Radical leaders design and are preparing for it." Johnson imagined he could parry this blow by crossing the party aisle and uniting whatever Republicans could be persuaded or compelled to follow him with the old Northern Democrats to create a new political coalition—a "third, or Tyler party"—with himself at its head.

This was not an impossible strategy. Democrats had managed to win more than three hundred thousand more popular votes than Lincoln in 1860, and then 45 percent of the presidential vote in 1864; they were still a force to be reckoned with—and clearly a force hostile to anything resembling black civil rights. "We want no Negro equality," Wisconsin Democrats exclaimed, as "it would degrade and brutify our race, giving Negro Husbands and Negro progeny to our fair daughters and sisters." A determined push-back by the president and a new bipartisan coalition to unseat the Radicals in the fall of 1866 elections might give Johnson the triumph he wanted, and the leadership of a new, postwar political world. At the prompting of Secretary of State Seward, on June 25 the *New York Times* published a call for "a National Convention, for the purpose of adopting…a platform of principles upon which the Northern and Southern States could take common political action."

The timing of the Johnson convention could not have been worse. By the time it met in Philadelphia on August 14, the fifteen members of the Joint Committee on Reconstruction, with the lofty William Pitt Fessenden in the chair, had finished recording six grueling months of witness examination and testimony from 144 individuals (ranging from Robert E. Lee to Clara Barton), and the published report they submitted on June 18 teemed with eyebrow-raising accounts of how the self-reconstructed states had done everything within their power to return the freedmen to little better than slavery. "Congress," the report soberly concluded, "cannot be expected to recognize as valid the election of representatives from disorganized communities" or "admitting such communities to a participation in the government."

As if on cue, white Southerners confirmed every bleak suspicion in the report in an eruption of race riots in Southern cities. For three days at the beginning of May, working-class whites in Memphis launched bitter and bloody attacks, first on mustered-out black soldiers whom they feared would become rivals for their jobs, and then at African Americans generally in South Memphis, which had drawn up to twenty thousand black fugitives during the war. It did not help Johnson's reputation that the federal commandant at Memphis, Major General George Stoneman, had been warned not to intervene "until orders are rec'd from Washington"—orders that had not been forthcoming. By the time Stoneman finally moved in to disarm the rioters, forty-eight black Memphians were dead and "every negro church and schoolhouse in the city" had been burned to the ground.

More rioting followed. In Norfolk, a freedmen's parade degenerated into a shoot-out that left two whites and two blacks dead. In June, Charleston was "disturbed and humanity shocked by serious and bloody riots, between white and colored citizens and troops." In July, rioting convulsed New Orleans. Since Louisiana already had a civilian state government in place at the time of Lincoln's death, under the governorship of James Madison Wells, Johnson allowed Wells to hold self-reconstruction elections in November 1865. But Louisiana had a larger share of Radical sympathizers than any of the other rebel states, and in June, they proposed to call the original 1864 state constitutional convention back to life in a meeting at the Mechanics Institute in New Orleans on July 30. Instead, a crowd of white police and suspiciously well-armed civilians tried to prevent the convention from taking place in the Institute, and a general melee broke out. By mid-afternoon, when federal troops at last arrived to restore order, 38 people had been killed and 146 wounded, most of them black Louisianans who been ruthlessly shot down by their attackers. It was, said federal Major General Philip Sheridan (who commanded the military district in New Orleans) "no riot; it was an absolute massacre by the police."

Johnson instantly accepted any explanations that blamed the violence on "the Radical members of Congress," but the country

3. On the morning of May 2, 1866, the city recorder urged the white citizens of Memphis to arm themselves and "kill every Negro and drive the last one from the city." That night, *Harper's Weekly* reported, "the Negroes were hunted down by police, firemen and other white citizens, shot, assaulted, robbed, and in many instances their houses searched under the pretense of hunting for concealed arms, plundered, and then set on fire, during which no resistance so far as we can learn was offered by the Negroes."

thought otherwise. Nothing was more "alarming in this sad affair," wrote E. L. Godkin of *The Nation*, than "the coolness with which he refrained from expressing one word of honest indignation at the slaughter." When the pro-Johnson Philadelphia convention met in August, the organizers did Johnson no service by inviting the two most notorious anti-war Democrats, Fernando Wood and Clement Vallandigham.

But no one was more capable of doing harm to Johnson than the man himself. Each member of Johnson's cabinet was invited to the Philadelphia convention, and Johnson made acceptance of the invitation a condition of remaining in office. Three of them—Attorney General James Speed, Postmaster General William Dennison, and Interior Secretary James Harlan—refused, and then resigned. Then, a week after the close of the convention, Johnson set off on what was billed as a political pilgrimage to Chicago to dedicate a monument at the tomb of Stephen Douglas. The notion of honoring the man who had twice opposed the martyred Lincoln was as close as Johnson could get to announcing his defection from the Republican Party. Johnson proceeded to turn each stop on his "Swing Round the Circle" into a stump speech against Radical candidates, thus racking up further cumulative political errors.

People who remembered Johnson's inaugural performance had good reason to fear that this was a mistake—and indeed it was. In Cleveland, Johnson lashed out at the Radicals as "this gang of office-holders, these blood-suckers and cormorants"; in St. Louis, he dismissed the New Orleans massacre as "substantially planned" by the Radicals and called for "the emancipation of the white men as well as the colored ones." Soon enough, his shotgun style attracted hecklers, and Johnson could not resist doing what they wanted him most to do, which was to descend into an insult match. When someone in the audience called out "Traitor!" Johnson shouted back, "I wish I could see you," continuing,

> I will bet now, if there could be a light reflected on your face, that cowardice and treachery could be seen in it. Show yourself. Come out here where we can see you. If ever you shoot a man, you will stand in the dark and pull your trigger...Those men—such a one as insulted me here tonight—you may say, has ceased to be a man, and in ceasing to be a man shrunk into the denomination of a reptile, and having so shrunken, as an honest man, I tread on him.

The cost of this behavior surprised Johnson: "the respect of the whole country and a hundred thousand votes." It was even more costly for his allies. Harvard students booed one of Johnson's apologists in Massachusetts, the venerable Robert C. Winthrop, at their commencement ceremony. As the congressional election tallies began to arrive in September, it was clear that

Johnson-affiliated candidates, at both the state and federal levels, had lost New England; the elections in Pennsylvania and Ohio in October were even worse. When the political bloodletting had finished, the Republicans in the Fortieth Congress would have five more seats in the Senate and six more in the House—and no reason in the upcoming final session of the Thirty-Ninth Congress to offer Johnson more than the frostiest welcome.

"If the President does not take the present terms," Iowa senator James W. Grimes gloomily informed Gideon Welles, "harder ones will be proposed." But Andrew Johnson was no more inclined to yield in defeat than he had been in victory a year before. He kept vetoing legislation of various sorts—bills covering everything from permission for a mining company to purchase public lands, to Colorado statehood—and Congress merrily proceeded to override them. Congress did likewise with Trumbull's civil rights bill two weeks after Johnson's veto. A new bill for the Freedmen's Bureau, guaranteeing to the freedmen "any of the civil rights or immunities belonging to white persons," was vetoed by Johnson on July, 16, 1866; this time around, the Senate and the House overrode the veto within twenty-four hours.

Relentlessly, Johnson kept banging his head against the Radicals' brick wall. In the annual message he sent to the second session of the Thirty-Ninth Congress in December, he criticized the failure "to admit to seats loyal Senators and Representatives from…States whose inhabitants…had engaged in the rebellion." The rebel states "are nothing less than States of the Union," he declared, and by refusing them recognition, Congress was standing in the way of "the revival of fraternal relations, the complete obliteration of our past differences, and the reinauguration of all the pursuits of peace."

How Johnson could expect anyone to agree after the Memphis and New Orleans shoot-outs defied comprehension. But he continued to delude himself with the advice of cronies who whispered that Johnson's troubles were only the product of a conspiracy "to thwart the President's great scheme of adjusting the Union." Ulysses Grant, now the general of the army, began to worry that Johnson would brand Congress as "illegal, unconstitutional and revolutionary." And there were vast rumors that Johnson was toying with the idea of preventing the Fortieth Congress from convening, after the pattern of the coup which brought Louis Napoleon to power in France in 1851, by employing the state militia of Maryland and putting "Maryland and the District of Columbia under martial law."

Nothing came of this plan, however, because Johnson was weaker than he realized. Beginning in February 1867, Congress swept control of Reconstruction entirely out of executive hands with a series of four Reconstruction bills. The first dissolved the self-reconstructed governments and imposed an overlay of five military occupation districts on the one-time Confederate states (except for Tennessee). In each district, commandants would exercise plenary military and civilian rule "to protect all persons in their rights of person and property, to suppress insurrection, disorder, and violence, and to punish … all disturbers of the public peace."

The second Reconstruction Act on March 23 made the commandants' principal responsibility the creation, for the first time in the history of American elections, of a registry of eligible voters whose qualifications—namely, that they had "never been a member of any State legislature, nor held any executive or judicial office in any State, and afterward engaged in insurrection or rebellion against the United States, or given aid or comfort to the enemies thereof"—ensured that no ex-Confederates could participate. Only those eligible voters who met these requirements would then elect delegates to state conventions, and write state constitutions which would entitle them "to representation, and senators and representatives"—but only if Congress agreed. The third and fourth Reconstruction Acts further defined how the commandants could unseat uncooperative civil officials, laid out schedules for the registration process, and established residency requirements.

Johnson, of course, vetoed each bill, raging that they placed Americans "under the absolute domination of military rulers." Congress overrode these vetoes, as well. Presidential-style Reconstruction was dead.

Chapter 3
Arrogance: March 1867–May 1868

For the survivors of the defeated Confederacy, the first issue was simple survival. The war had wrecked the Southern economy beyond most implications of the word "wrecked." "Financial ruin seems to be universal," wailed the South Carolina planter, Henry William Ravenel. "There was not a man in the place who was thirty years of age who had not fought in some capacity," wrote an up-country South Carolinian, "and there was not a woman who had not gone hungry for weeks and badly clad for years."

The losses were so great that the numbers cease to register. In what Walt Whitman called "the desolated, ruined South . . . nearly the whole generation of young men between seventeen and thirty" had been "destroyed or maimed; the rich impoverished; the plantations covered with weeds; the slaves unloosed and become the masters; and the name of Southerner blackened with every shame." Emancipation alone had wiped between $1.6 and $2.7 billion of capital investment off the books. Per capita income in the South collapsed by more than 40 percent, and real estate fell in value, ranging from an 18 percent loss in Tennessee to a whopping 70 percent devaluation in Louisiana. A third of Southern livestock and half of the South's farm machinery had disappeared, and with them, the agriculture that depended on them, as land under cultivation shrank by 34 percent in South Carolina and 30 percent in Louisiana. Banking capital, much of it invested in Confederate securities, suffered losses of 28 percent, sending interest rates on what remained for borrowing through the few intact roofs. Total direct and indirect costs—including the value of enslaved labor—were probably close to $13.6 billion—which does not even begin to convey the sense of demoralization that accompanied the losses. "The whole country is alive with robbers," shivered one Tennessee woman. "Every night we hear of a new robbery and sometimes murder."

No reconstruction would succeed which left the former Confederacy an impoverished shell, and victorious Northerners thought they knew exactly the sort of new economy that needed to be substituted for the old one. The great Republican goal of abolishing slavery was not entirely a crusade to right a racial injustice; abolishing slavery was not, in fact, much of a racial question at all, but rather an economic one. "I see National glory in the future such as the past has never seen," rejoiced Benjamin Brown French, and not just because slavery is "forever abolished," but because the South would soon be "thriving under Free labor & Free rule! No more Cotton lords, but plenty of Cotton Commons, and all the land pouring out its productions & becoming immensely rich!" The Union "represents the principles of free labor," declared a New York pamphlet, and only when "the victory of the Northern society of free labor over the landed monopoly of the Southern aristocracy" was complete would the war be over.

> The United States is truly the land—the very paradise of labor.... Even capital, which in Europe controls labor, here becomes subordinate to and serves labor. It is the free and intelligent labor of the country that creates the Administration or the Government.... Whatever may be said against the doings and intrigues of the politicians, yet it is the highest honor of the system of government of the United States that Free labor—that is to say, the equal right of all men to the pursuit of happiness—has been recognized as the first natural and inalienable right.

In the most basic sense, "free labor" was simply a shorthand term for liberal economic democracy, of the same sort advocated by the "Manchester School" in Great Britain and by liberals in France, Italy, and Prussia in the mid-nineteenth century. Among free labor's fundamental tenets were the encouragement of small-scale manufacturing and industry, especially through government-sponsored "internal improvements" (in the form of canals, highways, and railroads); economic mobility, with constant movement up the ladder of classes; and the practice of a constellation of bourgeois virtues—such as thrift, prudence, industry, religious faith, temperance, rationality, and nationalism—which would thus dignify those whom the *New York American* described as "the enterprising mechanic, who raises himself by his ingenious labors from the dust and turmoil of his workshop, to an abode of ease and elegance" and "the industrious tradesman, whose patient frugality enables him at last to accumulate enough to forego the duties of the counter and indulge a well-earned leisure."

In the eyes of free-labor Republicans, the mistake of the South had been to allow the thousand-bale planters to turn the Enlightenment clock back, toward what was essentially a replica of medieval serfdom. "Who knows," the *New-York Tribune* had once asked, "but we may see revived there the feudal tenures—maiden-right, wardship, baronial robberies, the seizure of white children for the market, military service, and the horrible hardships of villenage which men have fondly deemed forever abolished." In the South, the ruling class of "monarchists and aristocrats" had shunned government-sponsored improvements, cultivated a style based on braggadocio, and held poor whites and black slaves in the grip of a permanent and oppressive hierarchy. "There labor has been degraded," the *Chicago Tribune* lamented, "the laborer left untaught...thus converting half the Union into a charnel house of despotism, without a free religion, free speech, free press or free schools."

The war, however, had swept this "despotism" away, and the ash heaps that dotted the Southern countryside were blessings in disguise, since they could now be cleared for Northerners to introduce into the South a New England-style high type of culture—what Republican periodicals like the *Continental Monthly* described as "the cultivated valley, the peaceful village, the church, the school-house, and thronging cities." The South "under the old system" was "adverse to manufacturing and commercial enterprises." But now, the South's "worn-out plantations will become thriving farms, its mines and inexhaustible water-powers will call into play the incessant demand and supply of vigorous industry and active capital."

Reconstruction would thus have twin aims: a "reconstruction such as will protect loyal men, black and white, in their persons," but, added Frederick Douglass, one which will also "cause Northern industry, Northern capital, and Northern civilization to flow into the South, and make a man from New England as much at home in Carolina as elsewhere in the Republic." In John Greenleaf Whittier's vision, Reconstruction would

> The cruel lie of caste refute,
> Old forms remould, and substitute
> For Slavery's lash the freeman's will,
> For blind routine, wise-handed skill;
> A school-house plant on every hill,
> Stretching in radiate nerve-lines thence
> The quick wires of intelligence;
> Till North and South together brought
> Shall own the same electric thought,
> In peace a common flag salute,
> And, side by side in labor's free
> And unresentful rivalry,
> Harvest the fields wherein they fought.

This was a vision captured by Thomas Nast's famous cartoon, "Emancipation," whose ten vignettes hopefully pictured the full integration of the freedpeople into a middle-class future. Here was a bourgeois revolution—not in the Marxist sense of being a necessary footstool to the "real" proletarian revolution, but an end in itself, as the triumph of rights and liberal democracy, an Enlightenment counterrevolution against what the Northern middle classes feared was the real wave of the future: namely, the renascence of oligarchy and monarchy.

The principal obstacle to realizing this dream was the refusal of the defeated Southern planter class to admit that it had been defeated. Whatever else had been lost, title to Southern lands remained in the hands of the same landowners who had owned them before the war. In western Alabama's "Black Belt," 236 landowners possessed at least $10,000 in real estate in 1860 (with the median landholding amounting to 1,600 acres); by 1870, 101 of those landowners were still in possession—which was about the same rate of persistence over time that had prevailed before the war. They, too, had lived by an ideology, but one composed of Romantic medievalism, Jeffersonian agrarianism, white supremacy, and a general suspicion of bourgeois ambitions. "The typical Southerner," warned a contributor to the *Atlantic Monthly*, "possessed a...cast of character which was founded mainly on family, distinction, social culture, exemption from toil, and command over the lives and fortunes of his underlings." Free labor meant nothing to the planter, since "it is the highest gentility in him not to work," and one Northern reporter believed that "nine-tenths of the people must be taught that labor is not debasing."

If Johnson was fool enough to issue them a free pass, Frederick Douglass warned, Southerners would simply default to the prewar order of things, even after the ratification of the Thirteenth Amendment at the end of 1865, and especially if they were allowed to remain in possession of the lands they had owned before the war. "Slavery is so strong that it could exist, not only without law, but even against law. Custom, manners, morals, religion, are all on its side everywhere in the South." Everything was governed by a pervasive and "rigid spirit of caste." Black codes simply exchanged the legal reality of slavery for what Georgia planter William Hodgson called a "state of serfage or ascription to the soil." In Georgia, "colored people are not allowed to travel without passes from their former owners, while others still are afraid to acknowledge themselves free. In many places their meetings are broken up, and schools strictly forbidden...while in others murder and other horrid outrages are the ordinary suffering of our people....Several who worked for a share of the crop were driven off, as soon as it was gathered."

Worst of all, the great landowners seized on the Johnson amnesty to reclaim the lands the army had confiscated during the war and turned over to the freedmen. In 1865, William Tecumseh Sherman (through Special Field Order No. 15) set aside a thirty-mile-wide belt of four hundred thousand acres of prime rice- and cotton-growing land along the Georgia and South Carolina coast for forty thousand freedmen; in North Carolina, the military department commander ordered chaplain Horace James to "take possession of all unoccupied lands" on Roanoke Island "and lay them out and assign them...to the families of colored soldiers...and other blacks in the employ of the Government"; around Fortress Monroe in Virginia, contrabands simply set up for themselves on land abandoned by Confederate owners. "The colored man is not content when given simple emancipation," lectured John Mercer Langston, "he demands...to acquire, hold, and transmit property."

The end of the war, however, brought back the refugee landowners, and when they attempted to enforce legal title and evict the freedmen, angry confrontations ensued. George Benjamin West came home from the Confederate army "without a cent of money," found "30 axemen" cutting wood on his father's land "for Jerry Lee, a slave of my sister's," and chased them away.

Elizabeth Allston's mother revisited her South Carolina plantation to demand the keys to the barns from the freedpeople who had occupied them. She had almost persuaded "the head man" to surrender the keys when a "young man who had stood near, with a threatening expression sprang forward and shouted, 'Ef yu gie up de key, blood'll flow'...and a deafening clamor followed." The "head man" paused, then "returned the keys to the depths of his pocket." On Edisto Island, in the Sherman Reserve, a group of landowners who tried to evict black squatters were told, "You had better go back to Charleston and go to work there, and if you can do nothing else, you can pick oysters and earn your living as the loyal people have done—by the sweat of their brows." On St. Catharine's Island, black farmers organized by a former hotel waiter named Tunis Campbell armed themselves to prevent the island's owner from regaining possession "and would not allow any white person to land." In the lowlands of southern North Carolina, a mixed-race farmer named Henry Berry Lowry and a small band of fighters struck back at white landowners, raiding farms and disappearing into the swamps of the Pee Dee and Lumber Rivers.

It did little good. Samuel Thomas, who had commanded the Sixty-Fourth US Colored Troops during the war and in 1865 was named a Freedmen's Bureau commissioner in Vicksburg, Mississippi, warned that Southern whites "still have the ingrained feeling that the black people at large belong to the whites at large," and "to take property away from a negro they do not consider robbery." The Roanoke Island freedmen lost control of their colony in 1866, and most of the freedmen moved away. Tunis Campbell was expelled to the Georgia mainland, and within ten years had been imprisoned on trumped-up charges. The Sherman Reservation shrank under lawsuits for reclaimed titles, until it amounted to no more than one-fifth of the original set-aside.

It did not help, either, that the freedpeople, at this early stage, had no press to advertise their needs or the injustices inflicted on them. Nor was there a large fund of politically experienced black leadership ready to take up the freedpeople's banner. In South Carolina, Robert Smalls made headlines during the war by boldly piloting the steamboat *Planter* right past the noses of Charleston Confederates and into the hands of the US Navy; in Florida, Josiah Walls had served in the Thirty-Fifth United States Colored Troops; John Mercer Langston was born in Virginia, educated at Oberlin College, and actually won election as one of the first African American public officials in Ohio in 1855. But in many other places, black political leadership was condemned to emerge slowly, and in the teeth of white hostility as well as intra-racial jealousies and suspicion. "In such a contest," sighed Mississippi's first black congressman, John Roy Lynch, "they were neither organized nor armed.... They and their white allies were entirely at the mercy of their political adversaries."

If they could not defend their land, the freedmen found other ways to assert themselves. The one most often employed was simply to leave, especially for the towns and cities. Before the end of April, five thousand freed blacks were crowding into Montgomery, Alabama, and when Union soldiers "advised them to stay with their old masters," they only replied, "No, da was going to be free." A Boston correspondent near Macon, Georgia, discovered an old freedman living in a small hut, and when he found that the man had been born in Tennessee, the correspondent was curious to know why the man had come so far for so little. "I likes to be a free man," the old man replied, "whar Ise can go an' cum, an' nobody says not'ing."

Those who did stay behind nevertheless wanted nothing more to do with "the servile arts." Confederate general and would-be congressman Cullen Battle thought that James Alston, "when he belonged to me...was quite an orderly negro." But since then, Battle was amazed to find Alston had become "exceedingly turbulent and sometimes...over-bearing...and insolent in his manner toward white people." The Georgian, Frances Butler Leigh (the daughter of the celebrated English actress Fanny Kemble), was furious to see that "their whole manner was changed: they took to calling their former owners by their last name without any title before it…and tried speaking to me with their hats on, or not touching them to me when they passed me." Black women were particularly irritating to Southern whites, since "the women do not like to work—it is not ladylike."

The most remarkable improvisation of the freedpeople was the school. Northern abolitionists had been dispatching teachers as "missionaries" to runaways and contrabands since the first such contrabands had shown up at Fortress Monroe in 1861. By the end of the war, the American Missionary Association, the American Freedman's Union Commission, and the Methodist Freedman's Aid Society had become launching pads for teachers who endeavored to teach basic literacy and numeracy skills to children and adults alike. "The pupils in Northern seminaries might often take a lesson from the pains with which these colored students…put into immediate use the lessons of the class-room," wrote Helen Ludlow, a teacher in the schools surrounding Fortress Monroe. In New Bern, North Carolina, "nearly a thousand joyfully accepted the privilege" of Freedmen's Bureau schools. Hostile whites "chased and stoned" teachers and pupils, but by 1866, there were 965 bureau schools across the South.

But nothing weakened the desire to own land. What the freedman wanted most, said Martin Delany, the black abolitionist, "is a home—one that he can call his own, and possess in fee simple." And the only agency likely to override the disaster of Johnson's amnesty and the truculence of the self-reconstructed state governments would be Congress.

This was exactly what Congress now proposed to do with the four Reconstruction bills it passed between February 1867 and March 1868. Andrew Johnson vetoed three of them; Congress overrode the vetoes and Johnson allowed the remaining bill to become law by refusing to respond, and the process of dissolving the self-reconstructed governments began. The Arkansas legislature adjourned on March 23, 1867, just as the Second Reconstruction Act was passed, and never reconvened; in Mississippi, the newly appointed commandant of what was now the Fourth Military District, Major General Edward O. C. Ord, allowed the state legislature to remain in session, but nothing could be done by it without his approval. With President Johnson's blessing, the Pierpont legislature in Virginia kept on sitting, too, but any further elections were suspended by the new commandant, Major General John Schofield, on April 2, and state offices were to be filled by military appointment.

The commandants, however, were merely a means, rather than an end. Under the terms of the Reconstruction Acts, their principal task was to create an entirely new electorate in the South that carefully excluded recusant Confederates and their sympathizers among the white population, and certified the enfranchisement of the freedmen through the creation of vast registries of eligible voters. Major General John Pope began his registration program only a week after taking command in Georgia, dividing the state into forty-seven election districts and creating three-man registration boards (each was required to include two whites and one African American) to publish lists and issue certificates of registration. Pope's boards certified 188,000 voters in Georgia (as opposed to the 106,000 who voted in the 1860 presidential election), almost equally split between black and white; in Alabama (which also belonged to Pope's Third Military District), 165,000 voters were certified, split unevenly between 104,000 black voters and 61,000 white voters. General Ord completed registration in Mississippi by the beginning of September, certifying 106,000 voters in the state, 60,000 of them black. In South Carolina, 121,000 voters were recorded, with previously voiceless black South Carolinians now accounting for 79,000 and with black majorities in twenty-one of thirty-one election districts. Taken together, the registration process would identify 1.3 million voters in the five military districts—and to the horror of white Southerners, 700,000 were black, with black majorities in five states.

Registration, in turn, was the signal for organization. In Georgia, the Freedmen's Bureau encouraged the creation of the Georgia Equal Rights Association, with its own weekly newspaper, the *Loyal Georgian*, and a host of "associations . . . in every town and neighborhood for the relief of [the] poor and suffering, and to see after the education of our children." In North Carolina, a statewide convention for a State Equal Rights league was called in October 1866. Union (or Loyal) Leagues, modeled after the wartime urban political organizations which had supported the Union war effort, appeared in Alabama and Mississippi "and gave the negroes their first notions of parliamentary law and debating," as well as a taste of fighting back by creating Unionist para-military militias "to murder or drive out . . . every man who sympathized with the Confederate cause."

The leagues then formed the foundation for organizing state Republican parties. Republican (or "Union") political conventions had met in Louisiana in 1865 and in Virginia in 1866; now, they sprouted biracial conventions in South Carolina a week after the passage of the first Reconstruction bill, in Houston in April, in Atlanta in May, and in Jackson, Mississippi, and Raleigh, North Carolina, in September. By October 1867, Republicans were congratulating themselves that "there are forty thousand white men enrolled in the Leagues, and these, with the blacks, will give us the state in perpetuity if we are only wise."

Unfortunately, they were too eager to believe. The principal defect of the Reconstruction Acts was that the five military districts were military, and thus presided over by commandants who had to be appointed by the president, given his position as commander in chief. Just how ready Andrew Johnson was to use this appointment power to his own ends became evident from the commandants he appointed: Ord, in the Fourth District, had once commanded black troops in the Army of the Potomac, but privately despised the Union Leagues and discouraged the freedmen's political gathering; John Schofield, in the First District (comprising Virginia), was convinced of "the absolute unfitness of the negroes, as a class" for "an equal voice with ourselves in Government"; Pope, who had threatened to close down all-white juries in Georgia, was abruptly removed from command in December 1867, and replaced by Major General George G. Meade, the hero of Gettysburg who was nevertheless utterly unsympathetic to the cause of black voting rights.

Philip Sheridan, who was installed at the head of the Fifth District (Louisiana and Texas), originally owed his appointment more to the concern of his chief and mentor, Lieutenant General Ulysses Grant, for the possibility of war in Mexico to depose the French puppet emperor, Maximilian. Once in charge of the Fifth District, Sheridan acted swiftly to remove Louisianan officials whom he held responsible for the Mechanics Institute riot, starting with the mayor and police chief of New Orleans, twenty-two members of the city council, and finally the attorney general and the governor of the state. "Game was scarce down that way then," Sheridan sarcastically remarked, "and some gentlemen amused themselves by shooting negroes....I stopped this sport and they loved me not." Johnson, likewise, quickly tired of Sheridan, and in August 1867 moved to replace him with Major General Winfield Scott Hancock, one of the most unapologetic Democrats in the Union army.

Congressional Radicals had long suspected that Johnson would use his military authority to undermine the Reconstruction Acts, and Johnson did nothing to discourage the rumors by ordering the creation of a new military district to include the District of Columbia. "If I should have trouble with Congress," Johnson had once asked Ulysses Grant, "whose side would you support?"—a question loaded enough to confirm every suspicion the Radicals had about Johnson's plans for a coup. On the same day that Congress passed the first Reconstruction bill, it also overrode a presidential veto of a Tenure of Office Act, forbidding the president to dismiss civil servants "until a successor shall have been in like manner appointed and duly qualified...with the advice and consent of the Senate," and then adopted an army appropriations bill that compelled the president to issue all orders to the army through the commanding general.

Sheridan was not a civil servant, but he did enjoy at least the limited protection of the army appropriations bill. So Johnson had to order Grant to perform the dismissal of Sheridan, which Grant was very reluctant to do. Only after arguing with Johnson and warning the president that Sheridan was "universally, and deservedly, beloved by the people who sustained this government through its trials," did he finally obey.

Sheridan was only one target. At the same time, Johnson charged straight at the Tenure of Office Act by "suspending" his increasingly uncooperative secretary of war, Edwin M. Stanton, and replacing him with Grant as interim secretary. Grant, who by now wanted nothing to do with anything that looked like cooperation with Johnson, tried to decline, and when the Fortieth Congress assembled on December 2, it quickly became clear that they would disallow Stanton's suspension. On January 14, 1868, with ill-concealed relief, Grant surrendered the keys to the War Department and Stanton returned to his office. Infuriated, Johnson ordered the adjutant general of the army, Lorenzo Thomas, to evict Stanton. The temperamental secretary instead barricaded himself in his office, defying repeated summonses from Thomas to surrender. In the end, though, it was Johnson who surrendered. On February 21, John Covode of Pennsylvania rose in the House of Representatives to offer a resolution, that "Andrew Johnson, President of the United States, be impeached of high crimes and misdemeanors."

4. On March 4, 1868, Chief Justice Salmon P. Chase presided as the impeachment trial of Andrew Johnson opened in the Senate chamber. "A large crowd filled the galleries and corridors, making the trial a public spectacle."

Congress had used its impeachment powers (under Article 2, section 4, of the Constitution) on only five occasions; only twice had the House of Representatives ever considered impeaching a sitting president, and those discussions had been, in an eerie parallel, about John Tyler in 1843 and (by motion of the same John Covode) James Buchanan in 1860. But Radicals in (and beyond) Congress had been talking about impeaching Andrew Johnson for two years. "The president should long ago have been impeached," declared *The Nation* in 1866, and Ohio representative James Ashley made repeated motions for impeachment in January and March 1867. But the Radicals were not able to persuade the rest of the Republican caucus to trigger a constitutional crisis until Johnson, by sending Thomas to replace Stanton, clearly defied the Tenure of Office Act.

"The country was buzzing with rumors of iniquities which Johnson was meditating and would surely attempt if he were not disarmed," remembered Carl Schurz. "There was a widespread feeling among well-meaning and sober people that the country was really in some sort of peril." Grudgingly, the reluctant yielded. After three days of "excited eloquence" and a final damning speech by Thaddeus Stevens, while "a driving storm of hail and sleet" raged outside, the House impeached Andrew Johnson on a straight party-line vote of 126 to 47. But Stevens and the House managers of the ensuing trial in the Senate were unable to elevate Johnson's disregard of the Tenure of Office Act to the level of "high crimes and misdemeanors." By April, it was clear that the Senate would fail to convict, and on May 16, the Senate was unable to muster the necessary two-thirds majority to convict Johnson of the primary charge. Ten days later, the remaining charges also fell short.

Andrew Johnson had survived, but barely, and his presidency, even with ten months remaining in his term, was from that point on as good as over.

Chapter 4

Resistance: May 1868–March 1869

The year 1868 should have been the high moment of achievement for Reconstruction. The four Reconstruction Acts reversed the disastrous self-reconstruction initiatives of 1865, and Andrew Johnson had been resoundingly rebuked, if not actually convicted, by an impeachment trial. The Southern states, politically purged of disloyal whites and abundant with freedmen primed to assume a major role, now proceeded to organize a new round of state conventions (known with unintended humor as the "black-and-tan" conventions), which would write a new round of state constitutions, guaranteeing a new order of free labor and liberal democracy in the old Confederacy.

In Alabama, Republicans easily dominated the state convention called under General Pope's oversight. Ninety-six of the 100 delegates were Republicans, and 18 were black. The convention's president, Elisha W. Peck, was born in New York, moved to Alabama in the 1820s, and was forced to flee the state for Illinois during the war. Mississippi's new convention met in January 1868, with 97 delegates, all but 18 of them safely Republican, and chaired by Beroth Eggleston, a transplanted Ohioan and former Union general. North Carolina's convention also met in January, and also with a lopsided Republican majority, 107 to 13, 15 of whom were black.

The fall of 1868 would also mean another presidential and congressional election season. It was clear that Andrew Johnson had no political future with the Republicans, but few Democrats were eager to welcome him back to the party's ranks, much less nominate him for a second term. A few Tennessee admirers put his name up at the Democratic national convention in July anyway, but after twenty-two ballots the Democrats nominated former New York governor Horatio Seymour, and Johnson ended the convention with only four votes. "I have experienced ingratitude so often," he complained, still in self-crucifixion mode, "that any result will not surprise me."

Like John Tyler before him, Johnson had become a pariah in the eyes of both parties. Meanwhile, the Republicans had the strongest possible presidential candidate waiting in the wings: the war-winning general Ulysses Grant, who had been edging closer and closer to the Radicals as Andrew Johnson grew nearer and nearer to impeachment. When the Republican National Convention went to balloting for a nominee, there was no question that "there is not one loyal heart," declared the New York state delegation, "that does not beat in unison with the sentiment that calls upon us to select that great chieftain." Grant was unanimously nominated by all 650 delegates, "with swinging hats and waving handkerchiefs" and a spontaneous chorus of "The Battle Cry of Freedom," and went on in November to win the presidency by 300,000 votes and a 214 to 80 victory in the electoral college.

Even before the election, congressional reconstruction was bringing Southern states back into the Union, this time firmly under Republican control. Between June 22 and July 15, Congress readmitted seven of the ten rebel states—Florida, Georgia, Alabama, Arkansas, Louisiana, and North and South Carolina—under new constitutions. South Carolina's constitution enfranchised any "resident of this State" who was also a "male citizen of the United States, of the age of twenty-one years and upwards...without distinction of race, color or former condition," and forbade the state legislature from passing "any law that will deprive any of the citizens of this State of the right of suffrage, except for treason, murder, robbery or dueling, whereof the persons shall have been duly tried and convicted." And there was serious discussion of appealing to the federal government for a loan of $1 million to be used in buying land for the freedmen. "There is but one way to make a man love his country," argued Franklin J. Moses, an ex-Confederate who had transformed himself into a Radical Republican, "Give them lands; give them houses."

The most startling aspect of the new state governments was the role played by African Americans. Of the eighty-four Republicans in the lower house of the Georgia legislature, twenty-nine were black. In Arkansas, eight were black, and the average age was thirty-seven; five were biracial, three were ministers, three were farmers, and one was a postmaster. Florida elected fifty-three members to its lower house, thirty-seven of them Republican, and of those Republicans, seventeen were African American. In North Carolina, sixteen African Americans were elected to the state House of Representatives and three to the state Senate. As a group, they impressed a *New York Times* correspondent as possessing "by long odds the largest share of mental calibre." By contrast, "there is scarcely a Southern white man" sitting in the state offices "who has character enough to keep him out of the Penitentiary."

Only a little less startling were the numbers of Northerners who heeded the call for a culturally transformed South and reinvented themselves as missionaries of free labor. John Townsend Trowbridge, a journalist who journeyed through the South in 1865, warned that converting the white population to free labor principles would be an uphill battle. He found it "impossible for the people of Mississippi—and the same may be said of the Southern people generally—to understand the first principle of the free-labor system." For generations, Southern whites had been taught to believe that labor was "beneath the dignity of a gentleman." But Reconstruction, wrote Albion Tourgée, now offered a means of refashioning the entire labor system of the South—provided the South was "desouthernized and thoroughly nationalized" by importing a new white population to replace the old planter class and act as missionaries of the free labor cause.

Reconstruction by State

States reconstructed under the Reconstruction Acts	Readmitted to the Union
Arkansas	June 22, 1868
Florida	June 25, 1868
Louisiana	June 25, 1868
North Carolina	July 4, 1868
South Carolina	July 9, 1868
Alabama	July 14, 1868
Virginia	January 26, 1870
Mississippi	February 23, 1870
Texas	March 30, 1870
Georgia	July 15, 1870

Tourgée was an example of how eager Northerners were to help this process along. Born in Ohio and educated in New York, Tourgée had served in an Ohio regiment, endured the sufferings of Richmond's Libby Prison as a prisoner of war, and settled in Greensboro, North Carolina, at the end of the war in order to find relief in a warmer climate for a wound that had damaged his spine. He opened a law office and became president of a small wood-handle business, the Snow Turning Company, whose success left him "perfectly thunderstruck at the profits," as well as the good wages paid to its largely black workforce. John Hay, who

5. Civil rights legislation under congressional reconstruction admitted blacks to jury service in southern states alongside whites for the first time. The *New York Times* observed: "The sensation is peculiar ... to see a Court in session, where former slaves sit side by side with their old owners in the jury, where white men are tried by a mixed jury, where colored lawyers plead, and where white and colored officers maintain order. But this is done at every Court, and justice is not overwhelmed."

had been Lincoln's private secretary, was another example. Hay had been sent in 1864 to register Southerners willing to take the oath of allegiance, and came away sufficiently intrigued by Florida ("It is the only thing that smells of the Original Eden on the Continent") that he bought land to grow oranges near St. Augustine. Albert T. Morgan, who had been a student at Oberlin College at the war's beginning and served in the Second Wisconsin at Gettysburg, had a vision of "a tide of thrifty emigrants and others with capital settling southward," and within twenty-five years making "the two million people of the Mississippi lowlands twenty millions, and in a century a hundred millions." Even Harriet Beecher Stowe, the author of *Uncle Tom's Cabin*, bought orange groves near Jacksonville, moved South, and created a free-labor colony around the village of Mandarin.

Disgruntled Southern whites stigmatized the free-labor apostles as carpetbaggers, a nickname that sprang into usage in late 1867, after the first of the "black and tan" conventions met in Alabama, to describe a Northerner "who turns up here and there and everywhere," like a cheap valise made from carpet remnants in-hand, "ready to run for office or to do any other job that will pay expenses." Nevertheless, this Northern free-labor vanguard supplied twenty-eight of the fifty-one white delegates to South Carolina's constitutional convention in 1868 and another thirty-eight to the one hundred delegates at Alabama's constitutional convention. The new governors of Georgia (Rufus Bullock), Louisiana (Henry Clay Warmoth), and South Carolina (Robert K. Scott) were Northerners; of the two hundred office holders appointed by Governor Harrison Reed in Florida, fifty were Northern-born, and Reed himself had only arrived in the state in 1865. "We are, in fact and from absolute necessity, transplanting the whole South with the higher Civilization of the North," rejoiced Frederick Douglass. "The New England schoolhouse is bound to take the place of the Southern whipping post."

In hindsight, it is clear that it all happened too fast. Little more than a year elapsed between the passage of the Reconstruction Acts and the readmission of the first seven Southern states, and during that time, voter registration had to be carried out, the old Confederate power structure dismantled or disabled, state constitutional conventions called and constitutions written, and elections held for both state and federal legislatures—not to mention a presidential election as well. In the absence of any clear blueprints for rebuilding an entire political order, much was going to be overlooked, and the overlooking would provide uncertain foundations for further rebuilding. Worse, in the welter of political reordering, little was done to address the problem of land ownership, the restructuring of commerce, or the reorganization of public resources.

Not that the new state governments would get much direction from the national executive. Andrew Johnson continued to stick stubbornly to the path of noncooperation, vetoing bills until his last day in office, issuing a blanket amnesty to former Confederates on Christmas Day 1868, and declining to participate in his successor's inauguration. At least there was little more harm Johnson could do by that point, apart from writing a stinging farewell address that described the Reconstruction Acts as a "catalogue of crimes" against the Constitution. His Christmas "universal amnesty and pardon" would only relieve the last ex-Confederates (including Jefferson Davis, still under indictment for treason but free on bail since 1867) of federal criminal penalties; the political exclusions written into the new state constitutions would remain in place.

Much greater difficulties were generated by fumbles in the actual implementation of the new Reconstruction regimes. For one thing, the exclusions in the Reconstruction Acts were intended to remove large numbers of disgruntled and disenfranchised ex-Confederates from political participation, but the registration process proved easy to game and most of the military governors indulgent. Only 14 state officials from self-reconstruction out of 342 were removed in Arkansas, and only 12 in North Carolina. In 1860, 62,000 votes were cast in the presidential election, all of them, of course, by white voters; in 1868, the total number of registered whites had shrunk to only 57,000, alongside 47,000 new black voters. White Louisianans had tallied 50,000 votes in 1860; the number of registered white voters in 1867 sank only to about 45,000, beside 84,000 black Louisianans.

But those ex-Confederates sidelined by the registration process could still find ways to bring public attention to their political positions. In Georgia, unbowed Democrats met to denounce "the effort to establish the supremacy of the negro race in the South, and to place the destinies of those states in the hands of adventurers and irresponsible persons," and nominated the ex-Confederate General John B. Gordon (who had taken the Johnson oath in 1865) for governor. The Republican nominee, Rufus Bullock, defeated Gordon, 83,000 votes to 76,000. But it was worth noticing that in 1860, a total of 116,000 votes had been cast by white Georgians, which meant that Bullock had been elected largely on the strength of black voter turnout, and that 48 percent of the reconstructed Georgia electorate had chosen his opponent. Not that white Republicans always proved steadfast, either: no sooner had Georgia Republicans taken control of the Georgia legislature than, with the connivance of the military commandant, George Meade, they turned away three black state senators and twenty-nine black representatives on the flimsy assertion that the state constitution made no provision for black legislators; in Arkansas, the state constitutional convention

THE TWO PLATFORMS.

The Democratic Platform | The Republican Platform
Is for the White Man. | Is for the Negro and the Carpet-Bagger.

6. The New York Democratic party distributed this campaign card to white voters during the 1868 presidential election. It advised "White Men of New York" that "the Republicans, in Convention, declared in favor of Negro Suffrage," that "they want Negro children to be educated in the same schools with White Children," and "have exempted from taxation the Bonds of the rich [as] class legislation."

enfranchised black voters but then debated criminalizing interracial marriage.

A more direct problem was created by the determination of Southern whites to impose a kind of counter-disfranchisement on blacks through intimidation. In a hierarchical society, honor had always been a volatile component of politics, and Southerners displayed a cultural weakness for a rush to the sword whenever honor was challenged. Whipping, rape, starvation, and murder had long been the chief means of controlling nearly four million slaves, whether it was the routine application of physical punishment by owners or overseers, or the slave patrols organized from slaveholders and non-slaveholders alike to stop and investigate blacks found, for any reason, off the plantation. And, the war itself had immersed numbers of Southerners in guerrilla warfare, partly against Union forces but just as often against each other, and brought new recruits to a long-time strategy for settling regional differences across the South.

The practices of patrolling for slaves and guerrilla warfare now passed easily over into terrorism. "If persecution and confiscation are to follow," Confederate clerk J. B. Jones heard one Confederate official prophesy in 1865, "instead of organized armies we shall have bands of assassins everywhere in the field, and the stiletto and the torch will take the place of the sword and the musket—and there can be no solid reconstruction." With over half a million paroled Confederate veterans at large—mostly unemployed and smoldering with resentments—large pools of clandestine white resistance easily sprang to life: the White League and the Knights of the White Camellia in Louisiana, the Society of Pale Faces in Tennessee, the Regulators in Florida, and the Constitutional Guards in Virginia. They made no effort to conceal their intention to recapture control of their states by white Democrats. The mission of the White League, as "the white man's party," was to "rescue Louisiana from the polluting embraces of ... a hybrid pack of lecherous pimps ... brought forth in pollution, nursed by filthy horbies, and dropped in Louisiana to show to the world to what depth of corruption, disgrace and infamy human nature can stoop."

Fresh riots broke out in Georgia, where five cases of Henry repeating rifles were used by local Democrats to attack a Republican rally in Camilla, killing nine, and in Louisiana, accompanied by over a thousand murders between November 1867 and Election Day in 1868. In St. Landry Parish, in the town of Opelousas, between two hundred and three hundred blacks were killed, and black prisoners in the parish jail were marched out and executed. "The negroes all over the Parish have been disarmed, and have gone to work briskly," rejoiced a Democratic newspaper. "Their loyal league clubs and been broken up" and "St. Landry is quiet for the first time since the War."

The tactics of these white resistance groups could include economic bullying as well as political violence. "Thousands of negroes had liens on their crops released, land rented them at nothing, supplies promised for next year, or money paid them outright in consideration of their turning democrats, or of staying away from the polls," reported the *Atlantic Monthly*. Those who could not be bought could be ruined, and at election times, "the torch began its terrible work all over the country." Likewise, white Northerners who employed freedmen—and who were thus drawing black Southerners away from labor peonage under the old masters—could find their properties and improvements reduced to cinders in the night, or their workers waylaid and beaten to force them back to the cotton fields.

The most infamous of these white jacobins was the Ku Klux Klan, whose "night visits and whippings and murders was the legitimate offspring of the patrol." Originally organized in Tennessee in 1866 as a carnivalesque club with a Greek-style name similar to a fraternity (κύκλος simply means "circle"), the club's hijinks concealed a profound racial hatred of blacks and a determination to overthrow Reconstruction. The Klan quickly became, by 1867, a night-riding posse, complete with graveyard costumes, bizarre ranks and titles, and a mission (as Nashville editor S. C. Mercer described it in 1868) to "overawe union men, both black and white" and "put the negro in a semi-serf condition."

Despite their grotesque rituals and preposterous outfits (in Alabama, Charles E. Robert saw them wearing "a red gown, trimmed with white braid; pants of the same; high hat, with vail over the face; holes for the eye and mouth"), the Klan spread by both extension and imitation. Nathan Bedford Forrest, the rough-hewn Confederate general who had presided over the massacre of black soldiers at Fort Pillow in 1864, and who became the unofficial head of the Klan in 1867, estimated that the Klan could count forty thousand members in Tennessee and more than half a million in the rest of the South. In "small squads of masked men" or in battalions of "two or three hundred masked and mounted men," they broke into houses; shot, whipped, and raped the inhabitants; and warned any freedmen who "thought we were all free; that we could vote," that "we will stop all of that." In Tennessee, between three thousand and four thousand black refugees escaping Klan violence streamed into Nashville in 1868; on June 13, hooded Klansmen armed with pistols and ropes even hijacked a passenger train in Columbia, Tennessee, searching the cars for a Republican congressman.

It was hard to ascertain whom the Klan hated most: the freedmen, the carpetbaggers, or home-grown Southern unionists (who received their own title at the same time: "scalawags"). In most states, the scalawags were drawn from the tiny prewar Southern bourgeoisie—lawyers, journalists, physicians—and more often than not, they had received Northern educations. In Louisiana, out of 172 prominent unionists who turned Republican, 65 percent had been born in the North or other countries. Even though they had long resided in the South, to their unreconciled neighbors they were nothing but turncoats who had gone "over to

7. This Ku Klux Klan party was captured in eastern North Carolina in August, 1871, by Deputy US Marshal Joseph G. Hester as they were attempting to lynch "a strict and earnest" Republican, John Campbell. Hester had the group photographed in Raleigh so that "the people at large may know...what a Ku Klux tribunal looks like."

the republicans for the sake of office or plunder." But James L. Orr, who had once been Speaker of the US House and a member of the Confederate Senate, retorted that the South's past was nothing to be proud of, and that what he wanted for his home state of South Carolina was "the material prosperity of New England. I would have her acres teem with life and vigor and industry and intelligence, as do those of Massachusetts."

At least scalawags like Orr could claim some prior political experience; it was, in the end, inexperience which proved a deadlier poison in Reconstruction's cup than murderous white violence. Of the twelve carpetbaggers elected to Congress from Alabama, Louisiana, Mississippi, Texas, and Virginia, only one had ever held political office; all but two had been army officers who decided to stay in the South at the end of the war as merchants or landowners. Of the carpetbagger governors—Powell Clayton (Arkansas), Adelbert Ames (Mississippi), Rufus Bullock (Georgia), Harrison Reed (Florida), Henry C. Warmoth (Louisiana), Robert Scott (South Carolina), and Gilbert Walker (Virginia)—not a single one had previously been active in politics. This created a deep well of political amateurism, the mistakes of which would be held up as proof across the country of the political evil of the entire Reconstruction project and used to obscure the despotic behavior of Southern resisters. In Georgia, Rufus Bullock quarreled with John Emory Bryant, the president of the Georgia Equal Rights Association; the Mississippi scalawag governor, James Lusk Alcorn, tried to win over his one-time rebel friends, which brought him into direct conflict with the Maine-born Adelbert Ames. Louisiana's Republicans split over control of office appointments in the federal customs house in New Orleans, leading to the impeachment of Governor Warmoth, and the attempted assassination of Warmoth's successor, William Pitt Kellogg.

Inexperience also created manifold opportunities for factionalism, swapping political favors, and most dangerous of all, a willingness to seek alliances with ex-Confederates on the "the enemy of my enemy is my friend" principle. Corruption, too, was a problem: Florida's Republicans were "solid citizens," recalled black journalist T. Thomas Fortune, whose father sat in the legislature; but they also had "wide-open eyes to the main chance, which was not always reached by the straight and narrow, and much crooked business went on which helped to bring the Reconstruction government into disrepute."

Dominating all these political weaknesses was the political situation of the new president, Ulysses S. Grant. No one's reputation stood higher with Northerners after Lincoln's death than Grant's; "The election of Grant as President of the United

States" was seen by John Langdon Sibley as the occasion for "great rejoicings by the Republican party, in as much as it indicates a purpose to put an end to the unrighteous alliance of the Democratic party of the North with the rebel spirit at the South, which still lingers with the hope that this combination will again put the southerners in the political ascendance." Yet, even though Grant won the presidency with 58 percent of the popular vote, he lost New York by ten thousand votes, and New York City by sixty thousand votes. Five states had given him victory margins of less than 5 percent, and Democrats had gained twenty-two seats in the House of Representatives. Even where Republicans managed to hold seats in Congress, the margins of victory were unnervingly thin. Nor could it save some of Radical Republicanism's most favored sons. In Ohio, James Ashley (who had led the charge to impeach Andrew Johnson) was beaten with only 48 percent in his district, while Ashley's coadjutor in Radical Republicanism, John Bingham, survived by only 416 votes. Four governorships fell into Democratic hands; in Maryland, every state legislative district and all five US representatives went Democratic, while in New Jersey, three of the five congressional districts elected Democrats, and Democrats held the state legislature.

The Democratic Party was, in fact, already entering a period of recovery that turned out to be remarkable in its speed and extent, and both Northern and Southern Democrats would soon enough find common cause in shaking off the hated rule of Republicans. In another year, this would convince former Confederates to stop hammering their fists against Republican walls, and look instead to promoting fissures in Republican unity, and wooing the weak-kneed and disenchanted to some new banner.

Chapter 5
Distraction: March 1869–
May 1872

Ulysses Grant's 1868 presidential campaign slogan, "Let us have peace," was a study in vagueness—and not without reason, since Grant believed that "in times like the present it is impossible...to lay down a policy to be adhered to, right or wrong, through an Administration of four years." This was intended as a statement of flexibility, but it could also be read as an attempt to duck hard decisions. His inaugural address on March 4, 1869, was only 1,100 words long; nearly half of it was devoted to his goal of liquidating the national debt: "Principal and interest, as well as the return to a specie basis as soon as it can be accomplished without material detriment to the debtor class or to the country at large." He spent more time on promising "the proper treatment of the original occupants of this land—the Indians" than he did on "the question of suffrage" in the South.

The day after his inauguration, he sent his list of cabinet appointees to the Senate for confirmation, and the national gasp of dismay was almost audible. "The announcement of the Cabinet has caused a general commotion," declared the *Chicago Tribune*, and no wonder: his old political sponsor, Illinois congressman Elihu Washburne, was given leadership over the State Department, despite his reputation as "coarse, comparatively illiterate, a demagogue without statesmanship or enlarged views," and two political unknowns—Alexander Stewart, a New York multimillionaire, and Adolph Borie—were given the nod for treasury and the navy. At least, Grant nominated for attorney general the well-respected Massachusetts jurist E. Rockwood Hoar. But Borie was so little known that one editor burst out in frustration, "The Hon. Adolph E. Bovie [sic], Secretary of the Navy, is—is—well, who in hell is Bovie, anyway?" Stewart withdrew his own nomination on March 9; Borie was gone by June; and Elihu Washburne, after eleven days as secretary of state, resigned and was bundled out of the country as American minister to France.

"No one doubted that Grant's intention had been one of reform; that his aim had been to place his administration above politics," Henry Adams recalled. The real problem was with Grant himself. "Grant appeared as an intermittent energy, immensely powerful when awake." But "for stretches of time his mind seemed torpid," and at those times he appeared "simple-minded beyond the experience of Wall Street or State Street." Grant did not initiate policies so much as react to crises. Never having held political office before, he displayed a fatal naiveté about people and government and allowed his inner circle of advisors and secretaries to direct affairs until embarrassment over their corruption or their folly roused him to action. There was never any doubt that he was well intentioned, especially on the subject of the freedpeople's rights—he declared the protection of black voting rights to be "a measure of grander importance than any other one act of the kind from the foundation of our free government to the present day," and he was the first president to employ black diplomats (to Haiti and Liberia). Yet he could also be inert in protecting those rights until they were actually assaulted and utterly blind to the incompetence and dissimulation of the officials he appointed to public trusts. Grant was, in the unforgiving eyes of Gideon Welles, "a pitiable object, wholly unfit for his position, the duties of which he no more comprehends now, than when he was acting as porter in his brother's store in Galena, or carting wood in St. Louis."

On the day Grant was sworn in as president, Virginia, Mississippi, Texas, and Georgia were still under military rule, per the first of the 1867 Reconstruction Acts. Nor did it look like they would be making any significant steps toward restoration any time soon. In Mississippi, an election under self-reconstruction had installed former Confederate general Benjamin Humphreys as governor. The military governor under congressional Reconstruction, Edward Ord, kept Humphreys in place until a new constitutional convention could produce a fresh document, have it ratified by the registered voters, and hold elections. But already, anti-Republican resistance was stiffening. A convention of Mississippi Democrats meeting in Jackson organized themselves as the Democratic White Man's Party. They denounced the "nefarious design of the Republican party to place the white men of the Southern states under governmental control of . . . the African negro," and called "upon the people of Mississippi to vindicate alike the superiority of their race"—which they did, by rejecting the new state constitution, 63,000 to 56,000.

Meanwhile, the Ku Klux Klan tracked down Northern-born schoolmasters (Allen P. Huggins was whipped and warned to leave Monroe County in ten days), invaded courthouses (and killed the judge, E. L. Bramlette, in Meridian), and kidnapped uncooperative blacks (in Sumter County). The situation came so close to chaos that in the summer of 1868, Humphreys was unceremoniously evicted from the governor's mansion by military order and replaced by Adelbert Ames, a Maine abolitionist and the son-in-law of Benjamin Butler, who had infuriated Southerners with his strict occupation policies as military governor of New Orleans during the war, and encouraged fugitive slaves by welcoming them as "contraband of war." Ames went at his work with a vengeance, dismissing sixty sheriffs, seventy-two judges, fifty mayors, and even local constables. The state constitution was resubmitted, and James Lusk Alcorn, who had sat in the 1861 secession convention but was now (as W. E. B. Du

Bois described him) "the most advanced reconstructionist," was duly elected governor.

But instead of these confrontations signaling caution to him, Grant proposed to move ahead as swiftly as possible to restore the remaining Southern states. Although Reconstruction "has not met with the success in all particulars that might have been desired," as he conceded in his first annual message to Congress on December 6, 1869, "on the whole they have been more successful than could have been reasonably anticipated"—a judgment that might have surprised a number of people on the ground in the South. Nevertheless, Virginia's legislature, at least, had met all the technical expectations of Reconstruction, and thus was entitled once more to send representatives and senators to Congress. Texas and Mississippi were at that moment in the middle of holding elections, and Grant hoped that "the acts of the legislatures of these States, when they meet, will be such as to receive your approval, and thus close the work of reconstruction."

Grant might have had more difficulty in persuading Congress to readmit the last hold-out states had it not been for the changes Congress itself had undergone. The old Radical guard was still represented in the Senate by Zachariah Chandler, Jacob Howard, Lyman Trumbull, Charles Sumner, and Henry Wilson. But Benjamin Wade was gone—the Ohio legislature had been captured by Democrats in the 1867 state elections, which doomed his chances for reelection—as was old Jacob Collamer, who died in 1866, and William Pitt Fessenden, who died in the fall of 1869. In the House of Representatives, the single most Radical voice of them all was stilled with the death of Thaddeus Stevens on August 11, 1868. As one by one the veterans of the Radical struggle fell silent, the expectations for a radical Reconstruction shrank as well, and Grant himself became the new radical baseline. The *New York Herald*'s reporter noticed that, during the reading of Grant's message aloud by the clerk of the House of Representatives, "some one on the floor said, 'Well, that's radical enough.'" And indeed it was, under these new circumstances. On January 24, 1870, the House passed an enabling bill to readmit Virginia by a lopsided 136 to 58 vote; Grant signed it two days later. Mississippi followed a month later, Texas a month after that, and Georgia, at last, on July 15, 1870.

This should have marked the conclusion of Reconstruction, and officially, it did—except that the Republican governments in the Southern statehouses were fragile and unstable and led by political nonentities willing to do anything to retain their offices. In Georgia, Rufus Bullock forgot the promises he had made to black Georgians and courted alliances with Georgia Democrats; they, in turn, cheerfully used Bullock to obtain majorities in the Georgia legislature in 1870 and then moved to impeach him. Franklin J. Moses, the Speaker of the South Carolina House and later governor, was described by Josephus Woodruff, the clerk of the state senate, as "a blackmailer" with "no conscience"; Francis Cardozo, South Carolina's secretary of state and the first African American to occupy a state office in Reconstruction, was a man whom Woodruff said "nobody ever knew to keep his word." They were more incompetent than corrupt; and the corrupt among them were not more corrupt than the slaveholding regimes that had preceded them. But incompetence and corruption were not what the hour called for, and the political corner-cutting that seemed routine under prewar state governments was now denounced as unholy fraud by disenfranchised whites and Democrats.

The Republican South was also economically shaky. During the five years since the end of the war, the crusade for a free labor economy in the former Confederacy had barely taken its first steps. The South owned only 12 percent of the nation's mills and factories, and employed only 7 percent of its population as laborers in those establishments. Cotton agriculture remained, as it had been before the war, the producer of the republic's single most valuable export commodity (some 32 percent of all exports as late as 1889). And no wonder: while commodity prices for wheat, corn, and coal had operated (except during the war years) within fairly narrow ranges, cotton was selling above all its prewar highs; in Georgia, Alabama, Mississippi and Arkansas, cotton acreage and production expanded, employing a black labor force indistinguishable from that under slavery. Great Britain still bought 58 percent of the cotton it imported for textile manufacturing from the United States, and that would continue to rise through 1876.

Struggling to jump-start a New Englandized economy, Southern Republicans spent unprecedented amounts of money on internal improvements, including railroads, turnpikes, and public education. Alabama and Texas doubled their railroad mileage between 1866 and 1872; Arkansas, which counted only thirty-eight miles of railroad at the end of the war, had 258 by 1872. The number of elementary and secondary schools more than doubled in Mississippi, North Carolina, South Carolina, and Florida between 1870 and 1879; in Georgia, the number quadrupled.

But the railroads were not, as it turned out, a magic bullet. Construction costs for railroads fluctuated between $30,000 and $50,000 per mile, and new rail lines built on speculation folded as fast as they were finished. In the Natchez district, six new railroad companies were established in the early 1870s; all of them failed. Georgia's state-owned railroad, the Western & Atlantic, plunged the state into $750,000 worth of debt in two years. And the Ku Klux Klan, seeing the railroads as the agents of Northern free labor, made railroad repair shops and new construction sites the targets of murderous raids—not the least because the railroads hired freedmen. In North Carolina's Alamance County, the Klan accounted for twelve murders and fourteen arsons on railroad property in one twelve-month period.

Nor were the schools entirely successful. Literacy would be critical to the economic and political awakening of the freedpeople, and their Republican allies, in the form of the Freedmen's Bureau and the American Missionary Association (AMA) moved south even before the end of the war to open schools. But the resistance they met was intimidating. When the AMA's William L. Coan left Chelsea, Massachusetts, in 1865 to open a freedpeoples' school in Lexington, Virginia, he was assaulted at a train station at Gordonsville. Coan persevered, and opened an AMA school in Lexington for three hundred freedpeople of all ages. But he was constantly harassed, his landlady was forced to leave Lexington, and the school's meetings were disrupted by rowdy cadets from the nearby Virginia Military Institute. Once Southern states were legally reconstructed, the costs of education were shifted to the new Republican legislatures, but they were frequently unprepared to accept the fiscal burden the schools represented. In Southern states where no public schooling systems had existed before the war, the construction and staffing costs were staggering. In Mississippi alone, 432 schoolhouses were built in just the 1871–72 fiscal year; the teaching staffs alone numbered 4,800, and the overall cost for funding the Mississippi system was just over a million dollars. Nor were the schools always welcomed by African Americans who could ill afford to pay fees and teachers. "You preachers and teachers are hard on us," one old man complained to Charles W. Chestnutt, a teacher (and the grandson of a slaveowner who could have easily "passed" as white and later became a major American novelist). "You want us to pay you thirty or forty dollars a month for sitting in the shade, and that is as much as we can make in 2 or 3 months."

These investments left Republican governments in Southern states mired in debt—Louisiana, for example, held $2.2 million dollars in unfunded debt, tax receipts of only $4.3 million, and a budget deficit of $60,000. South Carolina was in even worse shape: it had $5.3 million in unfunded indebtedness and only $1.6 million in revenue. Only Georgia and Texas managed balanced budgets. The debt, in turn, added to the new tax levies of

Reconstruction's state Republican governments and gave further fuel to resentment among Southern whites.

And as if these were not obstacles enough in the path of a new culture of free labor, there was always the intractable problem of race. Former slaveholders, thanks in large measure to the Johnson amnesties and the failure to break up or confiscate Confederate property, were thus free to use cotton profits to maintain a version of the plantation system and force the freedpeople into peonage; this, in turn, gave white Democrats the power to control black voting; and control of voting would spell the end of Republican governments and free-labor economics, and, as a Vermont journalist put it, "keep the negro in his condition of ignorance, that they may retain him as nearly as possible in his old state of slavery." Major General John Pope, who briefly supervised the Third Military District (comprising George, Alabama, and Florida) warned Grant that it would not take much before "the Union men & Freedmen" were reduced to being "the slaves of the old negro rebel aristocracy."

"The relation of master and slave no longer exists here," wrote one Mississippi valley planter, "but out of it has evolved that of patron and retainer." Nor were Republicans at all successful in appealing to small-scale Southern white yeomen, since the tax burden for schools, railroads, and infrastructure which, before the war, had been carried by taxes on slave ownership, now fell onto the shoulders of the small farmers and drove them into supporting the cotton elite. "Here and there through all the cotton states," marveled *Harper's New Monthly Magazine*, "are reappearing the planter princes of old time, still lords of acres though not of slaves." Slavery might have been dead, but it was only being replaced by hutted serfdom. "General," read a petition from the freedpeople of Edisto Island to Otis Howard, "we want Homesteads. . . . We can only do one of three things Step Into the public road or the sea or remain on them working as In former

time and subject to their will as then." This might be
emancipation, but it "is not the condition of really freemen."

The Southern Republican regimes might have had a better chance
if the federal government could have suppressed the most direct
threat to their survival, which was the violence, political
intimidation, and terror inspired by the Ku Klux Klan and its
fellow travelers among the White Leagues, Red Shirts, and Pale
Faces. "In my state since emancipation," complained Jefferson
Long, Georgia's first black congressman, "there have been over five
hundred loyal men shot down by the disloyal men there, and not
one of those who took part in committing those outrages has ever
been brought to justice." Even if "we take the men who commit
these outrages before judges and juries," added Long, "we find that
they are in the hands of the very Ku Klux themselves who protect
them." Although the Klan had been active in Tennessee, Arkansas,
Alabama (where Edmund Pettus was its "dragon"), and
Mississippi, it generated particularly violent collisions in North
Carolina and South Carolina in 1870. South Carolina's Republican
governor, Robert Scott, wrote to Grant in horrifying detail of
"colored men and women...dragged from their homes at the dead
hour of the night and most cruelly and brutally scourged for the
sole reason that they dared to exercise their own opinions upon
political subjects." Scott called out the mostly black state militia to
ensure peaceful voting in the October 1870 state elections. But a
day after the election, a pitched battle broke out in Laurens
County between the militia and 2,500 armed white Klansmen,
followed by still more fighting in Spartanburg, Union, and York
counties.

The prospect of what the *New York Herald* called "the lawless and
malignant elements of the late rebellion" on the rampage stirred
President Grant into action. Grant first called the newly elected
Forty-Second Congress into emergency session on March 4, 1871,
demanding that the Speaker of the House, James G. Blaine, focus
Congress's attention on "the single subject of providing means for

the protection of life and property" in South Carolina. Grant then issued a cease-and-desist proclamation on March 24; when that seemed to make no impression, he declared nine South Carolina counties to be in a state of insurrection, and suspended the writ of habeas corpus. Congress, likewise, passed a series of three Enforcement Acts that guaranteed federal protection for those seeking "to become qualified to vote without distinction of race, color, or previous condition of servitude," authorized the deployment of federal troops, and permitted individuals suffering harms to recover damages in federal court.

The federal government also had the advantage of being served by a tenacious attorney general, Amos Akerman (a former Confederate who had succeeded Judge Hoar in June 1870 and vigorously pursued the Klan for crimes in Louisiana and North Carolina), and a veteran solicitor, David T. Corbin, as federal district attorney. Akerman and Corbin wasted no time at all in obtaining 785 indictments and going to trial in the federal district court in Columbia, South Carolina. "The courts are going on here," Akerman jubilantly announced, and "There is trepidation everywhere." Or almost everywhere: the pursuit of the Klan induced a certain *schadenfreude* among black Republicans. "There is not one in fifty of them now but is uneasy and trembling at the sight of an officer or a blue-coat," chuckled Elias Hill, a Baptist preacher who had been beaten by the Klan, "and they are staying out in the woods by day, and some by night, like we used to."

Still, even in the face of federal authority, the Klan found ways to resist. Corbin was able to obtain only five convictions at the first round of trials in Columbia; he managed twenty-eight more at the next session of the district court in Charleston in April 1872, but only nine more in the third round back in Columbia the following November.

The volume of prosecutions strained Akerman's budget so severely that he had to turn down a US marshal's request for $200 to hire

8. Large numbers of free blacks gathered in Taylor County, Georgia, to vote in the 1868 elections, only to be turned away "on account that the voters (colored) had not paid their poll tax.... The whole crowd inside of the election room, the canvassers, challengers, or what their name may be, were composed of real Southern democrats, and their action a mere farce."

a detective. Worse still, Grant fired Akerman in December 1871 (Secretary of State Hamilton Fish had complained that Akerman had the Klan "on the brain"), and although his replacement, George H. Williams, continued to press for convictions in Klan cases across the South, the costs of the anti-Klan initiative were mounting. In 1872, Williams instructed Corbin to enter a *nolle prosequi* ("do not prosecute") in his remaining cases "for the sake of the public good." Nevertheless, the convictions Akerman and Corbin did manage to obtain under the Enforcement Acts allowed Grant to declare victory over the Klan insurgency—and turn his attention to other insurgencies that required reconstruction.

By 1870, Arizona, New Mexico, Utah, Idaho, Montana, and Wyoming all had territorial governments, and Kansas, Nevada, and Nebraska had been admitted to the Union as states. The wartime Homestead Acts unloaded publicly owned land there at fire-sale prices, often without much regard for the arability of lands where average rainfall fell undependably short of what was needed to sustain commercial agriculture. Nevertheless, settlers began moving into the new lands, and railroads laid track to open conduits to markets, beginning with the completion of the transcontinental railroad at Promontory Point, Utah, in 1869. Almost all of the financing of the railroads came through federal grants which were the virtual equivalent of the Homestead Acts—over 131 million acres west of the Mississippi. The chief hindrance to this expansion was the presence of the Plains Indians, who had been crowded westward by successive Indian removal campaigns between the Revolution and the Civil War. President Grant's impulses toward the Plains tribes were well-intentioned but paternalistic. "The Indians require as much protection from the whites as the white does from the Indians," Grant sharply observed in 1865. "My own experience has been that little trouble would have been had from them but for the encroachments & influence of bad whites." But at the same time, Grant's notion of protection included "placing all the Indians on large reservations" where "they will live in houses, have schoolhouses and churches, and will be pursuing peaceful and self sustaining avocations"—which, in a word, meant that they too would become part of the new world of free labor. While still general-in-chief, he invited Ely S. Parker, his military secretary and a Tonawanda Seneca sachem, to create a national inspection board to oversee and enforce treaties with the tribes. In 1869, Grant persuaded Congress to create a Board of Indian Commissioners "eminent for their intelligence and philanthropy," and in the summer of 1870, Grant took the unprecedented step of hosting a meeting in Washington with Red Cloud, the chief of the Oglala Sioux, and Spotted Tail, chief of the Brulé Sioux.

Still, little of what the commissioners recommended in their first report in 1869 would have struck the Plains Indians as especially philanthropic and the so-called Five Civilized Tribes of the Indian

Territory resented the suggestion that they were a racial problem similar to Southern blacks. (The Cherokee, in particular, complained that they were "vastly superior, in every respect, to any portion of the Negro race" and urged whites "to draw the necessary distinction between Indians and negroes.") Even Ely Parker dismissed the notion of signing treaties with the Plains tribes because "the Indian tribes of the United States are not sovereign nations capable of making treaties, as none of them have an organized government." Moreover, whatever effectiveness the commissioners hoped to exercise was undermined by squabbling within the board, accusations of corruption (which led to Parker's resignation and a congressional investigation in 1871), bickering over jurisdiction between the Interior Department and the War Department, and an ongoing rumble of tribal war involving the Utes, Comanches, the Chiricahua Apache, and the Sioux (which in 1874 erupted into full-scale warfare). Only the comparatively small numbers of the Plains tribes—fewer than four thousand Comanche, fewer than two thousand Pawnee, and fourteen thousand in the seven Lakota Sioux tribes—made it possible for the US Army to suppress Indian resistance in the West in ways it failed to do so in the white South, and even then, armed resistance did not subside entirely until after 1890.

The Grant administration had no more success in dealing with the Mormon enclave in Utah. Mormonism was one of the more peculiar offshoots of American religious enthusiasm in the nineteenth century, and one of the more successful once it established its own quasi-independent colony around the Great Salt Lake in 1847. It was governed as a Mormon theocracy, with its prophet, Brigham Young, acting as virtual dictator. Like slaveholders, free-labor Republicans raged against Young as an economic despot who "by espousing the interests of one class against those of the other, instead of attempting to reconcile them…introduced a new element of discord into his already inharmonious kingdom." But Mormonism offended bourgeois sensibilities even more with its espousal of polygamy, which the

1860 Republican platform had denounced as a gendered form of slavery.

Even while the Civil War was still in progress, Radical Republicans in Congress demanded that Utah be de-Mormonized "by force" and passed a statute in 1862 to ban polygamy "in a territory or other place over which the United States shall have exclusive jurisdiction." But again, budget restraints on federal prosecutors in Utah prevented aggressive action against the Mormon leadership. "Brigham Young is rich," complained federal district attorney George Bates, "but the US authorities are penniless." Utah remained a defiantly "Theo-Democracy" where "the petrified truth" is that the territory "is an absolute monarchy and Brigham Young is king." Meanwhile, calls for "the moral power of bayonets" to be used in subduing Utah were met with the same chill that was growing over the use of federal military intervention elsewhere. In October 1871, after a two-day fire devastated large portions of Chicago and generated "murder and plunder on all sides," federal troops were sent in to restore order without informing the governor of Illinois, John M. Palmer. The governor at once accused the Grant administration of reaching for "powers they did not possess, and that while free government endures cannot be conferred upon them." This delighted Democrats, who jubilantly insisted that what was good for the goose was good for the gander. "A northern State now tries her hand against usurpation," rejoiced one Southern newspaper, "We shall see whether circumstances alter cases." After all, "Governor Palmer is asserting only what we are asserting every day."

Grant's last insurgency was the only one he could be said to have triumphed over, and that was within his own party. Dissatisfied Radical Republicans who saw nothing in Grant but slow-footedness, and who suspected that Grant was using the Klan prosecutions and his penchant for appointing loyal nonentities to major federal positions to create a soft dictatorship, rallied around the call of Missouri's US senator Carl Schurz to dump Grant and nominate a "liberal Republican" replacement. Liberal Republicanism was largely an elite rebellion within the party ranks at the Radicals, whose racial egalitarianism they did not share and whom they blamed for the political chaos in the South. But even the Southern States Convention of Colored Men, which brought together the South's most prominent black leaders in Charleston, South Carolina, in October 1871, almost balked at P. B. S. Pinchback's motion to endorse Grant's reelection. Dissatisfied Liberals arranged to hold a national convention in Cincinnati on May 1, 1872, and assembled some of the bluest blood of Northern Republicanism: Charles Francis Adams, Lyman Trumbull, William Grosvenor, Morton Wilkinson, and Oliver Perry Morton. For many of them, the still-smoldering embers of the Chicago fire illustrated the error of Reconstruction's military ways. "The war of the rebellion is ended," said Ohio Judge Stanley Matthews in one of the convention's opening addresses, and "as the war has ended so ought military rule and military principles."

The problem in Cincinnati was that too many of the Liberal Republicans each imagined that they were best suited to receive the presidential nomination. The consensus heading into the Liberal Republican convention had been that Charles Francis Adams, the son and grandson of two presidents and the American minister to Great Britain during the war, ought to head the Liberal Republican ticket, with Lyman Trumbull as his running mate. But the platform committee was grievously divided, and Adams had no floor manager to round up delegate votes. On the sixth ballot, the convention nominated instead Horace Greeley, the editor of the *New-York Tribune* and one of the flightiest political minds in the country.

The nomination of Greeley—"the worst political fiasco ever enacted in American politics," snarled one Chicago newspaper— took the air out of the Liberal Republican movement even before the convention adjourned. When Schurz went to dinner afterward, a one-time Illinois political ally of Lincoln, Gustave

Koerner, remembered that Schurz first sat down at the parlor piano and played Chopin's funeral march. "The discontent with Grant was far-reaching," recalled George Frisbie Hoar (the brother of Grant's first attorney general), "but the nomination of Greeley was ludicrous and preposterous." In July, the Democratic national convention made an even more startling decision by endorsing Greeley, who was now running, in the scathing estimate of William Lloyd Garrison, as "a stool-pigeon for the Democracy to capture the Presidency." But there was never any serious hope that Greeley could prevail. It was, as *Harper's Weekly* described it, an act of "political suicide" by "a political assassin." Grant was unanimously renominated by the Republican national convention in June, and handily won reelection with 56 percent of the popular vote; Horace Greeley died three weeks after the election and won only three posthumous votes in the Electoral College. Republicans even gained back seats in the House of Representatives, increasing their majority to 203 seats.

For Grant, it was "my vindication"—but it would not last long.

Chapter 6
Law: 1866–1876

So much of Reconstruction is understood as a struggle over race, politics, and the nature of state sovereignty within a federal system that not enough attention is paid to the fact that it was also a constitutional struggle between the branches of the federal government. On the occasions when intra-branch conflict in Reconstruction actually does put in an appearance, it is usually in terms of the executive's clash with the legislature, whether in the figure of Lincoln versus Congress or Andrew Johnson versus Congress. The judiciary appears only in terms of isolated cases and their impact on the freedpeople's rights. But this incomplete analysis misses what is, in fact, a major part of the Reconstruction story.

The US Constitution apportioned various federal responsibilities among the three federal branches—executive (the presidency), legislative (Congress), and judicial (the federal courts)—but it did not do so evenly or with the same amount of detail. The Constitution gave the federal courts, beginning with the US Supreme Court, only the sketchiest of descriptions, and then, with a fine disregard for the separation of powers, left much of the construction of a federal court system in the hands of Congress. John Jay, sitting as the first chief justice of the United States from 1790 to 1795, wrote opinions on only four cases and "left the Bench perfectly convinced that under a system so defective it would not obtain the energy, weight and dignity which are essential...nor acquire the public confidence and respect which, as the last resort of the justice of the nation, it should possess."

John Marshall, the fourth chief justice, pushed back strenuously against both state overreach and congressional encroachment on the judicial branch until his death in 1835; his successor, Roger Brooke Taney, sat as chief justice for another twenty-eight years, and in the opinion Taney wrote in *Dred Scott v. Sanford* (1857), he overruled congressional authority to restrict slavery, even in the Western territories. If the executive and legislative branches could not solve the slavery question, then it was Taney's resolution that the judiciary would.

The case of *Dred Scott v. Sanford* aggravated the national temper over slavery, rather than soothing it. But when the Civil War broke out, Taney did not hesitate to give the courts primary oversight of how the war should be waged by insisting, in Ex parte *Merryman* (1861), that Lincoln had no power to deal with the rebellion by suspending the writ of habeas corpus. But *Merryman* was only Taney's opinion as a circuit judge, not a full Supreme Court decision, and Abraham Lincoln simply ignored it. More than that, Lincoln invoked the presumption of a set of "war powers" in the executive branch that justified an emancipation proclamation and a general suspension of habeas corpus. This rendered the Supreme Court nearly mute; if anything, its wartime decisions in the *Metropolitan Bank v. Van Dyck* (1863), Ex parte *Vallandigham* (1864), and *Prize Cases* (1863) tamely endorsed the administration's policies on paper money, military tribunals, and the US Navy's blockade of the Southern coast, respectively.

Nevertheless, Lincoln remained anxious that once the war ended, the rationale for emancipation which he had built around the "war powers" would evaporate, and a revived judiciary might attempt to dismantle what the executive and legislative branches had accomplished. "The emancipation proclamation," Lincoln wrote in

1863, "I think... is valid in law, and will be so held by the courts." But he could not be sure, especially with Taney as chief justice. So it came as a great relief to Lincoln when, first, Taney died in October 1864 and he was able to appoint the unquestionably pro-emancipation Salmon P. Chase in Taney's place, and second, Congress followed his promptings and passed a thirteenth amendment to the Constitution, banning slavery entirely and putting emancipation beyond recall by the federal courts.

Still, even though Lincoln was confident that Chase's appointment would render emancipation secure from the federal judiciary, Chase's tenure as Lincoln's secretary of the treasury had been marred by his unceasing schemes for self-promotion, and Lincoln feared "that if I make him chief justice, he will simply become more restless and uneasy and neglect the place in his strife and intrigue to make himself president." Lincoln was not wrong to suspect Chase's ambitions, for Chase almost at once began a campaign to rebuild the Supreme Court's damaged reputation and reassert the prestige it had enjoyed under Marshall and Taney. The Reconstruction federal courts, under Chase (and then Morrison Waite) as chief justice, would expand federal judicial oversight at the expense of state courts, reassert the centrality of habeas corpus (to the denigration of wartime military tribunals), enjoy an expanded control of the award of money damages through the creation of the Court of Claims, and give federal courts increased jurisdiction over bankruptcy cases (and through that, increased powers over the national economy). At the same time, the federal courts would also become, in the name of restraining overreach by the executive and legislative branches, a potent agent in the undermining of Reconstruction.

The federal court system at the end of the Civil War was not large. Nine justices sat on the US Supreme Court, but beneath them were only fifty-four federal district judges in as many districts. Appeals from the district courts were heard in ten federal circuit courts (a jurisdiction that combined several districts, where the local district judge and a Supreme Court justice for that circuit presided); in turn, appeals from the circuit courts went to the Supreme Court. The membership of the high court itself had undergone some serious reorganization. Alabamian John Archibald Campbell resigned his seat as an associate justice at the outbreak of the war, and was replaced by Lincoln's old friend and judge on the Illinois 8th Judicial Circuit, David Davis. Justice John McLean, who had dissented from Dred Scott, died on April 4, 1861, and was replaced by Noah Swayne of Ohio; Samuel Freeman Miller was confirmed by acclamation in Congress to replace a seat left vacant for two years by the death of Peter V. Daniel; and Stephen J. Field was appointed to a new seat on the court created by Congress in 1863. But the most significant change was at the very top, as Salmon Chase assumed the role of chief justice on December 15, 1864.

Originally a Democrat, Chase had risen in Ohio politics as a fervent opponent of slavery, to the point where he had been tagged as "the attorney-general for fugitive slaves." He moved to the Republican Party in 1855, and during the war he had agitated ceaselessly for a Radical Republican agenda in the Lincoln administration. Everything in his record suggested this would be the same path he would follow as chief justice. "It will hereafter be counted equally a crime and a folly if the colored loyalists of the rebel States are left to the control of the restored rebels," Chase warned Lincoln four days before Lincoln's death; merely "to confine the right of suffrage to the whites . . . will enable them to make all sorts of invidious and unjust discriminations; nor will they be slow to do so."

But Chase described himself as a Radical only "in principle, and [I] have never disclaimed the name; but I have tried to be a conservative in working." This was not because Chase was indifferent to black rights but rather because federal jurists lived with a distinction between civil and natural rights, which saw the federal government as responsible for defending specific constitutional privileges and immunities, but not the wider scope of natural rights. "Human Rights do not depend on the equality of Men or Races, but are wholly independent of them," declared the *New-York Tribune* in 1862, which is to say that they exist independently of statutes and codes and even constitutions. The US Constitution was therefore a hybrid document, in that it vested the protection of some natural rights in the federal government, but left the bulk of them—marriage, personal liberties—with the states, and it would be up to the states to recognize the freedpeople as a new class having claim to natural-rights protections. As Lyman Trumbull explained in the debates over the Freedmen's Bureau, "It is the policy of the Government that the rights of the colored men are to be protected by the States if they will, but by the Federal Government if they will not." But federal intervention was a secondary, compensatory step, not a primary one.

> The design ... is not ... to consolidate all power in the Federal Government, or to interfere in the domestic regulations of any of the States, except so far as to carry out a constitutional provision which is the supreme law of the land.... Let the people of the rebellious States now be as zealous and as active in the passage of laws and the inauguration of measures to elevate, develop, and improve the negro, as they have hitherto been to enslave and degrade him ... and we shall all be moving on in harmony together.

"So long as the states" did not attempt an explicit abolition of those rights, "the national government had no more power in the areas of traditional state jurisdiction than it had before the war." Not until states deliberately acted to deprive (or neglect protection for) those rights did the national government have the constitutional power to intervene.

Thus, the court would display a perfect willingness throughout Reconstruction to protect the freedpeople's property rights and physical safety when the states refused, but hesitate at enforcing equal access to streetcars, schools, and public spaces unless the states had clearly abdicated that responsibility, and not just as examples of criminal malice. Chase would also draw similar lines of jurisdiction between the branches of the federal government. He refused to preside in the traditional seat of the chief justice in the Virginia circuit courts because "it was neither right nor proper that the chief justice or any justice of the Supreme Court of the United States—the highest tribunal of the nation, and the head of one of the coordinate departments of the Government—should hold a court subject to the control or supervision of the executive Department." Even a justice as sympathetic to the Radicals as Samuel Freeman Miller felt it necessary to insist that "there can be no liberty where the power of judging is not kept separate from the executive and legislative powers."

The first test of postwar judicial assertiveness arrived quickly. In the fall of 1864, the commandant of the Military District of Indiana, Alvan Hovey, arrested a former candidate for the Indiana governor's chair, Lambdin Milligan, who had been part of a hare-brained, pro-Confederate plot to raise an insurrection in the Midwest. Milligan was duly arraigned before a military tribunal, found guilty of treason on December 18, 1864, and sentenced to be hanged. Milligan seems to have been persuaded that Lincoln (who delayed signing Milligan's death warrant) would issue a pardon, so it was not until after Lincoln's murder—and Andrew Johnson's mutterings about treason being made "odious"—that Milligan became nervous and petitioned in the US Circuit Court for the District of Indiana for a writ of habeas corpus, so that he could be retried in a civilian (and presumably less bloodthirsty) court.

Milligan's appeal for a writ was referred to the US Supreme Court, which heard arguments in March 1866 and announced a five-to-four decision in April. Written by David Davis (with a *caveat* from Chase), the decision discharged Milligan and declared military tribunals unconstitutional in areas where the civil courts were open and operating. "The Constitution of the United States is a law for rulers and people, equally in war and in peace," Davis wrote in ex parte *Milligan*, "and covers with the shield of its protection all classes of men, at all times, and under all circumstances."

Radical Republicans treated ex parte *Milligan* as a stab in the back, binding the ability of the army, and especially the Freedmen's Bureau, to intervene when Johnson's self-reconstructed regimes passed newer and more oppressive versions of the "black codes." A group of Radical congressmen wrote a series of articles for the *Washington Daily Chronicle*, protesting that "This opinion of the Supreme Court" shows a "total want of sympathy with the spirit in which the war for the Union was prosecuted," and offered a path by which Reconstruction could "be reversed by the very theory of construction which led to rebellion." Coming hard on the heels of Andrew Johnson's humiliation in the 1866 congressional elections, it now appeared that "there will be a new conflict," this time between Congress and the judiciary.

Such a showdown seemed all too likely when, in the same month the Milligan decision was released, the Chase Court moved to strike down "iron-clad" loyalty oaths ("iron-clad," meaning oaths which averred that the oath-taker would not only be loyal to the United States, but always had been). In January 1865, Missouri (one of the four slave states that remained loyal to the Union) adopted a new ordinance that outlawed slavery, but also added an oath to be taken by anyone acting in any public capacity, including clergy "of any religious persuasion, sect or denomination," that they had "always been truly and loyally on the side of the United States against all enemies thereof, foreign and domestic."

The Roman Catholic archbishop of St. Louis treated this ordinance as an unconstitutional trespass on religious freedom, and one of his priests, John A. Cummings, proceeded to say Mass and preach on September 3, 1865, without taking the oath.

Cummings was indicted, tried, and imprisoned. He appealed to the Missouri Supreme Court, then to the US Supreme Court, and in December 1866 the court branded the oath as a bill of attainder and an ex post facto law (because it imposed punishments for acts that "previous to the adoption of this Constitution...had not been declared punishable or illegal" and that had not been criminal at the time they were committed), violating the rule of presumption of innocence. This brought still more violent eruptions in Congress. "That supreme tribunal of justice has no power in the premises," declared Ohio congressman John Bingham. Reconstruction policies "are political not judicial questions, and can be decided only by the political department...and from that decision there is no appeal."

But Bingham needed more than fury to save Reconstruction from the hands of the courts, especially given that the Milligan and Cummings cases offered the possibility that the Supreme Court might send Lyman Trumbull's 1866 Civil Rights Act to the same dustbin. Bingham's solution, like Lincoln's on emancipation, was to cut the Gordian knot with a constitutional amendment that would place civil equality beyond the power of the courts to alter.

Bingham had proposed such a fourteenth amendment in December 1865, at the very opening of the Thirty-Ninth Congress. But it was not until after Andrew Johnson had vetoed Trumbull's Civil Rights Act (which Congress overrode) that Bingham's amendment was re-introduced, now expressly declaring that states were obligated to protect the "privileges or immunities of citizens of the United States." The Fourteenth Amendment was approved by the Senate on June 6, 1866, and by the House of Representatives the following week. But it took more than two years for the amendment to achieve ratification, partly because Andrew Johnson encouraged resistance to ratification at every point, and partly because the amendment itself was so awkwardly constructed. Of the amendment's five sections, only one dealt with the "privileges or immunities of citizens of the United States"; the others were an omnibus that forbade assumption of the Confederate debt, imposed a further ban on Confederate office holders, and threatened to proportion representation in Congress on the basis of actual voters (an indirect way to prevent Southern states from swelling their delegations in the House of Representatives on the basis of black citizens who were denied voting rights).

The weak link in the Fourteenth Amendment, however, was the failure of the amendment to specify just what was included in the "privileges or immunities" that the federal government now had authority to enforce. The court's 1823 decision in *Corfield v. Coryell* had narrowly defined the "privileges and immunities of citizens" (Art. 4, sec. 2) as simply matters of comity that states extended to citizens of other states; in 1833, John Marshall himself had declared (in *Barron v. Baltimore*) that the "privileges and immunities" clause was designed to restrict the federal government, not the states. So it remained possible that, even after the ratification of the Fourteenth Amendment, black voting rights could be kept at bay, since voting rights belonged to a category of rights over which the states, not the federal government, had primary jurisdiction.

The Fortieth Congress, assembling for its lame-duck session in December 1868, took up a resolution from the House Judiciary Committee, calling for a fifteenth constitutional amendment specifically to ban "discrimination...in the exercise of the elective franchise, or in the right to hold office in any State, on account of race, color, nativity, property, education or creed." This amendment was bitterly opposed by Border State Southerners who had never been subjected to Reconstruction, and by Northern Democrats who resented the extension of voting rights to African Americans in their own states. The lame-duck Republican majority settled for half a loaf, adopting a stripped-down version of the amendment that simply provided that "the right of citizens of the United States to vote shall not be denied or abridged by the

United States or by any State on account of race, color, or previous condition of servitude."

The Fourteenth and Fifteenth Amendments put the executive and legislative branches' shoulders to the wheel of voting rights, but they did nothing to prevent the Chase Court from digging potholes in their path, or chipping away at the severities of the Reconstruction statutes. In February 1867, Texas state authorities under the Reconstruction Acts brought suit against three brokers to recover US bonds that had been conveyed to Texas before the war as part of the financial settlement of Texas's affairs once it was annexed to the United States. In January 1862, the Confederate state of Texas authorized the sale of $634,000 worth of the remaining bonds to purchase stores and ordnance. But once Johnson's self-reconstructed Texas regime was in place, the state set out to recover the bonds from the brokers, George White and John Chiles, who had purchased them. If, as Lincoln had always claimed, the Confederacy was a legal nonentity, then the state regimes under the Confederacy could have no better claim to legal existence, and all transactions conducted under their aegis were as invalid as Confederate government debts.

But when *Texas v. White* landed in the lap of the Chase Court in 1867, the conclusion drawn by Chase was a good deal more complicated. Yes, Texas's secession was constitutionally invalid (which put paid, as far as any Supreme Court decision can, to all the elaborate arguments for secession). "The Constitution, in all its provisions," wrote Chase, "looks to an indestructible Union, composed of indestructible States." But Chase also drew a line of demarcation between invalid rebel actions like the bond sale, and the everyday transactions needed "to preserve the social community from anarchy and to maintain order." Whatever the Radicals' enthusiasm for a root-and-branch recreation of Southern society, "acts necessary to peace and good order among citizens…which would be valid if emanating from a lawful government must be regarded in general as valid," and neither

Congress nor the president had any authority to insert other substitute governments in their place.

Texas v. White was only the best known of the postwar claims cases that, in parallel with Andrew Johnson's amnesties, gradually gave back the legal ground that the Radical Republicans had claimed for reconstructing the Confederacy and presaged a more serious weakening to come—on civil rights and the Reconstruction constitutional amendments. Salmon Chase suffered a stroke in August 1872, recovering sufficiently to rejoin the court but dying after a second stroke in May 1873. In his place, the newly reelected President Grant installed as chief justice another Ohio lawyer, Morrison Waite. But it would not be Waite who called the court's tune. "Mr. Waite stands in the front rank of second-rate lawyers," snarled *The Nation*, and he was easily overshadowed by Samuel Freeman Miller ("the dominant personality now upon the bench") and Joseph P. Bradley (who joined the court in 1869).

The direction of the Waite Court was set by Miller even before the new chief justice took the oath of office. In 1869, Louisiana's Republican governor, Henry Clay Warmoth, signed legislation restricting New Orleans slaughterhouses to the use of a single state-chartered "grand slaughterhouse" in order to control the dumping of offal into the Mississippi River. The Butchers Benevolent Association balked, claiming that the new law would deny non-cooperating butchers the "privileges or immunities" bestowed equally on all citizens by the Fourteenth Amendment. But when the Supreme Court heard the butchers' appeal in 1872, Miller issued a majority opinion that (in April 1873) confined the application of "privileges or immunities" strictly to federal matters. "There is a citizenship of the United States," Miller wrote, which guarantees equal access to all the "privileges and immunities" the Constitution implies; but there is also "a citizenship of a state," and the two "are distinct from each other." The Fourteenth Amendment, Miller continued, protects only those "privileges and immunities" pertaining to federal citizenship, and only from interference by the federal government. The Louisiana statute interfered with neither; it governed only a function of state citizenship, which only the state could define.

Miller's intention in the *Slaughterhouse Cases* was an enlightened one—to allow Louisiana to prevent the contamination of New Orleans' water supply—and Miller explicitly criticized Southern whites' attempts to impose "upon the colored race onerous disabilities and burdens." But it also reinforced the Chase Court's proclivity for clipping the wings of Congress's federalization of "every little petty case of a civil character." And *Slaughterhouse* would have long innings in a case that began the same week, in the same state. In March 1873, black Republicans in Grant Parish, a Unionist Louisiana parish, occupied the county courthouse in Colfax to ensure that the newly appointed county sheriff, recorder of deeds, and police jurors were sworn in without challenge. On April 13, a hastily assembled white militia, 140 strong, attacked Colfax, setting fire to the courthouse and gunning down more than 150 blacks, many of them after they had surrendered to the whites. The federal district attorney for Louisiana, James Roswell Beckwith, energetically used the Enforcement Acts to indict ninety-eight of the Colfax massacre's participants, beginning with the ringleader, Christopher Columbus Nash, and his lieutenants, James and John Hadnot, William Irwin, and William Cruikshank.

However, the first trial of the Colfax defendants ended in deadlock before a mixed-race jury; a second trial in 1874 found only three of the defendants—Cruikshank, James Hadnot, and Irwin—guilty, and then only of conspiracy. When even that result was appealed to the Supreme Court as *US v. Cruikshank*, Chief Justice Waite concluded that the original indictments had no ground whatsoever. The crimes in Colfax were committed by private individuals against other private individuals in malice (not statute), and involved local Louisiana issues; the Constitution, including the Bill of Rights and the Fourteenth Amendment, protected the "privileges or immunities" only of people acting as US citizens, and only against official state encroachments.

The *Slaughterhouse Cases*, and then *Cruikshank* (in consort with *Blyew v. US* in 1872 and *US v. Reese* in 1876), hobbled the power of both the Enforcement Acts and the Fourteenth Amendment to protect individuals from the actions of other individuals, and in many cases, to protect individuals from the actions of the states if no clear intention to violate federal law, or misconduct by federal actors, was involved. But it magnified the authority of the federal judiciary, even as it rang hollow for many of the people who had hoped that the federal courts would enlarge their rights, rather than merely the court's. John Mercer Langston, addressing a protest meeting that also featured Frederick Douglass and former Mississippi senator Blanche K. Bruce as speakers, was infuriated to find "the Supreme Court...desirous of remanding us back to that old passed condition....How long must we wait for State action to give us our rights." The editor of the African American newspaper the *New York Globe*, T. Thomas Fortune, compared the court's decisions to being "baptized in ice water." "In the name of God, where now are the last two amendments to the federal constitution?" wailed the *Natchez Brotherhood*. "Will an American Congress permit a state to set up an oligarchy by reversing the intents and purposes of the organic law of the land?" Waite's intentions were traditional and circumspect and concerned themselves more with the authority of the federal courts to prevent other areas of government from overextension. But the Waite Court nevertheless created the beginnings of an arc that successor courts in the 1880s and 1890s, under Chief Justice Melville Fuller, would use to abandon civil protections for African Americans entirely. The eclipse of Reconstruction was at hand.

Chapter 7
Dissension: September 1872–April 1877

It has become an unwritten political assumption that second presidential terms are marked by a steady decline of presidential authority and an increase in presidential scandal. That was not necessarily the expectation in 1872, as Ulysses Grant entered his second term, but the four years that followed did a great deal to provide the template for that pattern. And the price Grant would pay for a rise in scandal and a concomitant decline of credibility during his second term would, in turn, accrue to the lasting harm of Reconstruction.

Grant survived a brush with scandal early in his first term, when two New York financiers, Jason "Jay" Gould and James Fisk, tried to use their connections to Grant's brother-in-law, Abel Corbin, to gain insider information on gold trading; he was embarrassed again by charges of corruption lodged against Ely Parker as commissioner of Indian Affairs in 1871. Grant had no direct involvement in either imbroglio, but the ooze of corruption fouled the political atmosphere all the same. Then, in September 1872, the *New York Sun* published revelations about Crédit Mobilier of America, the financial corporation that handled the subcontracting for the construction of the transcontinental railroad. On paper, Crédit Mobilier channeled the purchasing and contracting for the Union Pacific Railroad corporation; in reality, it was a dummy edifice that billed the railroads for its services at hugely inflated prices, while passing the profits back to Union Pacific's officers—and to twelve members of Congress, who accepted a bribe of shares in Crédit Mobilier and, in return, agreed to ignore Crédit Mobilier's shady dealings.

The Crédit Mobilier scandal did not touch Grant directly, but it set the wind blowing in a direction that did not bode well for him. Interior Secretary Columbus Delano had to be dismissed after charges of fraud were leveled at him; Grant's private secretary, Orville Babcock, was indicted for collusion with tax evaders; and Grant's secretary of war, William Worth Belknap, hurriedly resigned in advance of charges that he had taken bribes (only to have his replacement, George Robeson, charged with having profited from procurement deals for the navy). Before the Civil War, Mark Twain would write, "there was nothing resembling a worship of money or its possessor" among Americans. But the politicians and financiers "reversed the commercial morals of the United States.... The people had desired money before his day," but now they had been "taught... to fall down and worship it."

Twain, who was not guiltless of his own money-lust, was exaggerating at both ends of his recollections. The American world of the 1870s was still one in which more than half the manufacturing firms of a city like Boston employed fewer than seven laborers and a third employed fewer than twenty, where shop owners in Cincinnati "are generally men who are thoroughly acquainted with the practical features themselves. They are mechanics themselves." Lewis Latimer, who had enlisted in the Union navy at age sixteen, began work as an office boy, taught himself mechanical drafting, and assisted Alexander Graham Bell in patenting the telephone in 1876. Latimer's ascent could have been the textbook for the genius of free labor:

> He believed then that whatever a man knew he had put in a book, so when he saw the [draughts]man making drawings he watched to find out what tools he used, then he went to a second hand book

store and got a book on drawing and soon had a set of drawing instruments. He then looked over the draughtsman's shoulder to see how he used his instruments, and practiced with them at home until he felt thoroughly master of them, then one day he asked the draughtsman to let him do some drawing for him, the man laughed at him but finally consented to look at what he could do on another piece of paper and to his surprise found that Lewis was a real draughtsman, so he let him do some of his work from time to time and one day the boss saw him at work and was so pleased that he let him work everyday and gradually raised his wages so that from three dollars when he went to work he rose in eleven years to twenty dollars a week.

What Twain had right, however, was that the world of American finance had changed. The Civil War had caused a stampede of withdrawals from the American economy by European investors, a vacuum filled by an array of self-invented brokers, bond-sellers, and bankers—Jay Cooke, Jesse Seligman, George Higginson, Emanuel and Mayer Lehman, Junius S. Morgan, Jacob Schiff, Harvey Fisk, Alfred S. Hatch—many of them newly arrived immigrants who aroused the hauteur of both northeastern Brahmins and Southern julep-sippers. When the new financiers were caught distributing bribes and kickbacks to Grant's officeholders and his party, their follies fed a nativist xenophobia and achieved a visibility never before seen in American economic life. The ensuing revulsion fueled the Liberal Republican Party's insurrection in 1872, and it paved the way for Democrats to regain control of the House of Representatives in the 1874 elections for the first time in twenty years, trading a Republican majority of 114 seats for a Democratic majority of 61. Connecticut elected a Democratic governor and a Democratic state legislature; New York elected a Democratic governor, secretary of state, attorney general, and majority in the state assembly; Indiana and Massachusetts elected a Democratic governor; and New Hampshire and Ohio gave both houses of their state legislatures to Democratic majorities.

The stench of political corruption easily drifted over into Reconstruction, since it became easy to portray Southern whites as yet more long-suffering victims of the new-model financial rapacity. In 1873, James Shepherd Pike, a veteran abolitionist and associate editor of the *New-York Tribune*, began publishing "The Prostrate State: South Carolina under Negro Government," based on his own observations of South Carolina politics, as a serial for the *Tribune*. Pike's "The Prostrate State" was a sort of reverse *Uncle Tom's Cabin*, and it had approximately the same sensational effect. Standing in the state house in Columbia, Pike watched "old aristocratic society" replaced by a "Black Parliament" in which *arriviste* carpetbaggers and treacherous scalawags, in league with their black dupes, created a carnival of corruption: legislative appropriations intended to purchase land for the freedpeople ended up in the pockets of the politicos; a special appropriation was made to reimburse the speaker of the state house, Franklin Moses, for his losses on a horse race; taxes had risen by 500 percent since 1860, even as the value of taxable property in the state had fallen by a third; and the governor, Robert Scott, "spent $374,000 of the public money to get himself rechosen."

Pike's lurid account made no allusion to the prevalence of corruption in the South's prewar state governments, where "expert transfers of balances to undiscovered bournes" and "august defalcations" had been the order of the day. E. L. Godkin, the crusading editor of *The Nation*, simply concluded that the Republican governments of South Carolina and Louisiana were "a gang of robbers, making war on civilization and morality," and presidential intervention of the sort licensed by the Enforcement Acts was increasingly seen as just another species of corruption itself.

Not that Grant or Congress could have easily paid the public costs for such interventions after 1873, even if they had wanted to. The transcontinental railroad spun off a network of smaller trunk lines into vast stretches of the West, on the assumption that railroads would generate demand for their services by their mere presence. But of the seventy-nine major railroad lines in the United States in 1872, twenty-eight had never managed to pay a dividend to investors. On September 18, 1873, the banking house of Jay Cooke & Co., which had invested heavily in the railroads, ran out of money: it could not meet the demands of its depositors, and closed the doors of its Philadelphia and Washington offices. New York stocks dropped 10 percent and the *New-York Tribune* reported that "general demoralization...characterized the transaction of business in Wall-st." By the end of the month, 101 banks across the nation had gone under, dragging down savings and erasing pools of capital for investment. As the economy struggled and slowed, so did government income. Federal budget receipts fell by 13.5 percent between 1873 and 1875, while spending followed it downward by 5.5 percent. Thanks to the Panic of 1873, there would be less and less room to finance federal oversight of Southern affairs.

The Panic fed Reconstruction fatigue. "Let us have done with Reconstruction," the *New-York Tribune* cried in 1870, "The country is sick and tired of it....We cannot forever keep the boy out of the water because he has not learned to swim." Much of the political energy behind Reconstruction had been generated by the public backlash against Andrew Johnson in 1866 (which led to Lyman Trumbull's 1866 Civil Rights Bill and the Reconstruction Acts), and through the election of Grant, who was determined to ensure voting rights through the Enforcement Acts. But Northern Democrats had never despaired of recovering their prewar hegemony in Washington. They bitterly opposed the Fifteenth Amendment, and even after the amendment's ratification, they employed Klan-like intimidation to suppress black votes at the polls in Northern cities. In Philadelphia, the black civic leader Octavius Catto was shot to death at Ninth and South Streets by a Democratic assassin on the day of the 1871 Pennsylvania state elections.

Nevertheless, many Republicans remained dedicated to the possibilities of a new racial egalitarianism. "We believe the whole human race are one family," wrote Theodore Tilton in the *New York Independent*, and "we will have no permanent settlement of the negro question till our haughtier white blood, looking the negro in the face, shall forget that he is black, and remember only that he is a citizen." The Forty-First and Forty-Second Congress witnessed the arrival of six black congressmen (Benjamin Turner, Josiah Walls, Joseph Rainey, Robert Brown Elliott, Robert DeLarge, and Jefferson Long) and one black senator (Hiram Revels), elected by Republicans in Alabama, Mississippi, Louisiana, Florida, South Carolina, and Georgia. Overall, sixteen Southern blacks would serve in the Reconstruction Congresses; another six hundred would fill seats in state legislatures.

But for other Northern Republicans, black people remained something of an abstraction. "The Northern people," smirked Confederate War Department clerk J. B. Jones at the end of the war, "did not really like negro equality any better than we did," and John Emory Bryant was warned at the time he joined the Freedmen's Bureau that "the North is no more concerned for the African than the South." Even the staunch Radical Republican Benjamin Wade never rid himself of the habit of referring to black people as "niggers," and he complained that so much of the food in Washington was "cooked by Niggers" that "I can smell and taste the Nigger." Northern blacks were disproportionately concentrated in urban areas (61 percent in towns of over 2,500, 55 percent in towns of over 10,000), which meant that for many Northern whites, it was entirely possible to live most of one's life without ever meeting a black person. One member of the Arkansas constitutional convention in 1868 remarked that "I have seen, within fifty miles of St. Louis, the little children crowding the fence-rails, to look at a negro, and examining him with as much curiosity as if he had been a wild beast."

9. The murder of Philadelphia black political organizer Octavius Catto on October 10, 1871, from *The Trial of Frank Kelly for the Assassination and Murder of Octavius V. Catto* (1888). "Mr. Catto, having closed down his school, was passing down South street, between 8th and 9th streets, when he was approached by a white man.... Prof. Catto put his hand behind him as if to draw a pistol, when a car came up and he passed down the street a few paces.... Catto again advanced and attempted to cross the street, when the assassin leveled his pistol again and shot at him three times.... The first shot caused his death almost instantly."

It did not help, either, that the Northern free-labor apostles grew discouraged by the poor inroads they had made into Southern culture, and thus returned home disillusioned. They were, sighed a contributor to the *North American Review*, only "merchants, shopkeepers, mechanics, manufacturers, speculators, brokers, bankers" and not "barons after the fashion of the South." They were shunned and harassed, sometimes violently, "a fashion set by the aristocracy," said John W. DeForest, a transplanted Union army veteran and Freedmens' Bureau commissioner. John Richard Dennett, a correspondent for *The Nation*, discovered, "When I am known to be a Northern man...I am made to feel that my company is not desired"; a Southern physician sharpened the economic edge of Southern contempt by showing him a newspaper misprint—"Grand chance for Yankee enterprise and *thift*" (emphasis added)—which the doctor thought would have better read "grand chance for Yankee enterprise and theft." Harriet Beecher Stowe's colony in Florida, where she hoped to train "immature minds such as those of our negroes" to become a new version of "the laboring class of England," limped along, battered by white suspicion and unexplained arson, but Stowe's presence gradually diminished, until by 1884 she and her ailing husband left for good. Albion Tourgée lost his bid for a North Carolina congressional seat, and left his faltering law practice in Greensboro to write an embittered fictionalized memoir of his time in Reconstruction, appropriately titled *A Fool's Errand, By One of the Fools*. Having given up his hope of making headway for the "dignity of labor, in liberty and equality before the sovereign law" against the "feudal civilization" of the South, John Emory Bryant likewise departed Georgia for a new life in New York as a lawyer and realtor. The truth was, Benjamin Butler concluded, that "capital is timid":

> No man will risk his capital where he does not believe he can get Justice before a Jury; where he does not believe that the community would look favorably upon his enterprise; and where he does believe every advantage will be taken from him and every wrong done him. And he now believes all that in the Southern States....New England is dotted all over with men who have gone down to Virginia, and bought farms...and who have been absolutely driven out by their neighbors.

The Reconstruction governments contributed mightily to their own demise with their incessant, self-weakening infighting. "The Republicans are seriously weakened by faction," complained the *New-York Tribune*. "Their leaders charge each other with all manner of treacheries and misdemeanors." In Mississippi, Republican governor James Alcorn tried to establish alliances with both the freedpeople and poor whites, only to be undermined by Klan violence on one side and Radical criticism of his perceived soft-handedness on the other. When Alcorn was elected to the US Senate, his most vocal critic, Adelbert Ames, snatched the gubernatorial nomination from Alcorn's would-be successor, thus forcing Alcorn to enter the 1873 governor's race himself—which he then lost to Ames.

But Ames was himself embarrassed politically in December 1874, when Vicksburg's corrupt Republican mayor—"a white man at the time under indictment for twenty-three offenses"—was toppled by an alliance of reforming "White Liners." Emboldened, the White Liners marched on Vicksburg to demand the resignation of the county's black sheriff, Peter Crosby. A pitched battle between Crosby's black supporters and the White Liners broke out, and Governor Ames was forced to call on President Grant for federal troops to restore order. The following November, Ames again asked Grant for federal troops to ensure order during the state elections. This time, Grant hesitated. His newest attorney general, Edwards Pierrepont, warned that any further military interventions in the South would only play into Northern Democrats' plans to use the military "encroachments" accusation in the 1876 presidential elections. "The whole public was tired of these annual autumnal outbreaks in the South," Pierrepont advised Ames, and the Democrats were ready to use intervention "to condemn any interference on the part of the Government." That did not prevent white Democrats from intimidating voters with their own display of paramilitary force: John Roy Lynch, an African American congressman who had his Mississippi seat snatched from under him by clever redistricting, testified before a Congressional inquiry that in Jefferson and Claiborne counties, Democrats had organized themselves as "an armed military organization" and "would allow no republican meeting to be held and no republican speeches to be given by anybody." The result was a landslide for the Mississippi White Liners, and five months later, Ames resigned. The "terrorism was so intense," testified Lynch, "as in my judgment to make life, liberty, and happiness perfectly insecure except to democrats. I do not think there is any such thing as law in that society."

The same disastrous divisions sank the other Reconstruction Republican governments, one by one. Weakened by disputes between the Warmoth and Kellogg factions, and paralyzed by the Colfax massacre in 1873 and a fresh eruption of lethal race rioting in New Orleans in 1874, Louisiana wound up with two rival governors, one Republican and one Democrat, each demanding recognition from the federal government. Arkansas, similarly, ended 1874 with two rival Republican governors, Joseph Brooks and Elisha Baxter, and a Democratic legislature. Florida's Republican governor, Ossian Hart, skillfully managed to navigate between Florida's Republican factions and its unredeemed white Democrats; however, he died in March 1874, and in 1875 Democrats seized control of the state legislature. By the spring of 1876, only Louisiana and South Carolina still had Republican governments. "We have endeavored to protect law and property...by the force of provisional state, by the force of provisional congressional law, and by the force of the armies of the United States," Vermont Republican George Edmunds admitted, "and the result" has been that every tool had broken in their hands: "We have totally failed to secure the administration of justice."

End of Republican Reconstruction by State

States reconstructed under the Reconstruction Acts	Effective ending of Reconstruction
Virginia	October 5, 1869
North Carolina	November 28, 1870
Georgia	November 1, 1871
Texas	January 14, 1873
Arkansas	November 10, 1874
Alabama	November 16, 1874
Mississippi	January 4, 1876
Louisiana	January 2, 1877
Florida	January 2, 1877
South Carolina	April 11, 1877

But it was not Republican factionalism alone that crippled the Reconstruction regimes. The freedpeople themselves were anything but a political monolith, and they wasted political energy on internecine quarrels as vigorously as white Republicans had. The first fault line was the reluctance of Southern blacks to accept white Republican leadership as unquestioningly as whites had expected. Northern white schoolteachers found that Southern blacks did not want whites to run either their politics or their schools. The teachers from the American Missionary Association who descended on the occupied Port Royal Sound to educate and uplift the freedpeople discovered, as Austa Malinda French noted, that "nothing is more evident to those who actually know the Colored, than that while they respect, value, and revere, the good, they want little companionship with the whites."

Lawrence S. Berry, a freed slave turned journalist, urged his readers to "forget our sable complexion" and close ranks with progressive whites. But, as one Freedmen's Bureau agent discovered, "their long experience of slavery has made them so distrustful of all whites, that on many plantations they persist still in giving credit only to the rumors set afloat by people of their own color, and believe that the officers who have addressed them are rebels in disguise." Moreover, the freedpeople resented the paternalistic tendencies of well-intentioned whites, especially when assistance calcified into orders and sympathy into control. When Georgia's short-lived Republican legislature tried to ban the admission of black state legislators, black Methodist leader Henry McNeal Turner frankly said, "My colored friends, the white men are not to be trusted. They will betray you." And Hiram Revels, the first black US senator to be elected from Mississippi, denounced white Adelbert Ames and white Mississippi Republicans as "notoriously corrupt and dishonest," and actually applauded the downfall of Adelbert Ames as a triumph over "corruption, theft, and embezzlement."

But just as divisive were the fault lines that separated blacks from blacks. A racial hierarchy that bestowed privilege along a carefully graded spectrum of color had long existed in the black South. "There is in the Southern States a great amount of prejudice in regards to color," the African American abolitionist and novelist William Wells Brown admitted in 1867, "even among the negroes themselves. The nearer the negro or mulatto approaches to the white, the more he seems to feel his superiority over those of a darker hue." Louisiana's politics were more than sufficiently twisted by white factionalism, and made even worse by rivalries among factions led by Pinckney Benton Stewart Pinchback (one-quarter black, and married to a white woman), Oscar James Dunn (born a slave, to a slave mother and a free black carpenter), and Caesar Carpentier Antoine (a one-time business partner of Pinchback's, his father was a free *gens du couleur* and his mother was West Indian).

In postwar Savannah, Aaron Bradley mounted a political smear campaign against his rival for a seat in Congress, Richard White, a mixed-race Union army veteran from Ohio. White, sneered Bradley, was a "hybrid" who did not deserve the support of true African Americans. "What color will he represent himself?" asked Bradley, who then answered his own question: "The greasy color." Even Frederick Douglass and Martin Delany sparred, with Douglass (himself biracial) bitterly criticizing Delany's black racial purism for "going about the same length in favor of blacks, as the whites have done in favor of the doctrine of white superiority." Delany was right to assert African Americans' "need for dignity and self-respect," but not, Douglass warned, to the point where "he stands up so straight that he leans back a little" and ends up in a version of black racial triumphalism little different from white supremacy. Douglass also parted company with John Mercer Langston, despite Langston's agreement that "this is no more a white man's country and government than it is the country and government of the black man.... It is the country and government of the American people." Nevertheless, Douglass accused Langston of "mad political ambition."

These interracial feuds were a key factor in the most singular absence in black Reconstruction in the South: namely, the lack of a single commanding leader who could bind together the disparate threads of African American identity into a single movement. Slavery was certainly no useful training-ground for the game of politics, and the marginalized experience of free Northern blacks did not present much more in the ways of practical opportunities for honing political savvy. Given that only Louisiana and South Carolina had developed any substantial prewar populations of blacks who were property owners, business proprietors, and skilled craftsmen, the likeliest quarter from which such leadership could have developed was the Northern black community—but even then, few Northern blacks made the attempt. And no wonder; it was doubtful if Southern blacks would feel obliged to follow Northern leadership, a reluctance the National Conference of Colored Men demonstrated when it debated a resolution "That we pay no heed to such men as Fred. Douglass and his accomplices, for the simple reason that they are well-to-do Northern men who will not travel out of their way to benefit the suffering Southern Negro."

And it was certain that Southern whites would make aggressive Northern blacks a target of choice. "Write as you please, but *never go south*, or killed you *most assuredly* will be," warned Julia Griffiths Crofts, Douglass's British friend and supporter. "You are, in many respects, *a marked man*." So, when Douglass was invited to set up a newspaper in Alexandria, Virginia, in 1866, he politely declined: "It is not my duty to court violence or martyrdom or to act in any manner which can be construed into a spirit of bravado.... I think it wise to remain where I am, at least until the public mind of the South shall attain a more healthy tone than at present." Martin Delany and John Mercer Langston played highly visible roles as African American political leaders in the Reconstruction South, but those roles were plagued by division and distraction. Langston was only active in Reconstruction politics as an agent for the Freedmen's Bureau and the National Equal Rights League from 1865 till 1868, when he took up a faculty appointment at the new Howard University in Washington, DC. Delany grew so impatient with his white Republican allies in South Carolina that he accepted a judicial appointment from Democrats. "What benefit," he asked in 1874, "have the colored people in South Carolina derived from the propagation of Republican sentiments." None, in his estimate: "Such a party is not worth the effort to keep it in existence."

Charles Sumner might not have disagreed. Dumped by Grant and the Republican caucus from the chairmanship of the Senate Foreign Relations Committee, Sumner retaliated by leading the defection of the Liberal Republicans in 1872. He could sense a tidal wave of reaction heading toward Washington, and as his health deteriorated, he labored to persuade Congress to adopt a new civil rights bill. He died in March 1874, begging, "Don't let my bill fail"; the last session of the Forty-Third Congress passed it before the new Democratic majority in the House could assume power, but only by a tie-breaking vote in the Senate provided by Vice President Henry Wilson, and a disrespectful margin of 135–114 in the House, with 38 abstentions. It was Reconstruction's last hurrah (and would be duly overturned by the Supreme Court in 1883).

In June 1876, the Republican National Convention met in Cincinnati, and this time a plethora of candidates battled one another over the course of six ballots, until on the seventh, the convention settled on an outsider, whom *The Nation* deemed "a man by no means conspicuous in public affairs": Rutherford B. Hayes, a Union army veteran and second-term governor of Ohio. Hayes had loyally supported congressional Reconstruction and included black voting rights in his platform in his bid for the Ohio governorship. But by 1875, Hayes came to the conclusion that Reconstruction issues were costing him votes, and he backed away from endorsing Sumner's posthumous civil rights bill. The Democrats countered two weeks later with the nomination of Samuel Tilden, the reforming governor of New York, and almost at once the "outbreaks" Grant no longer felt eager to restrain with federal troops erupted in full force. The governors' races in Louisiana and South Carolina became violent referenda on Republican rule in those states. East Baton Rouge witnessed eighteen political murders in the month before the election. In Hamburg, South Carolina, an argument over right of way for a parade mushroomed into a skirmish between incumbent Republican governor Daniel Chamberlain's black militia and "Red Shirts" loyal to Democratic candidate (and ex-Confederate general) Wade Hampton; the fighting ended in the execution of four captured militiamen. Governor Chamberlain appealed to Grant for federal troops "to repress the violence in this State during the present campaign."

Grant, denouncing "the late disgraceful and brutal slaughter of unoffending men in Hamburg, S.C.," issued a cease-and-desist proclamation and sent in three companies of infantry. "The scene at Hamburg, as cruel, bloodthirsty, wanton, unprovoked, and as uncalled for as it was," Grant wrote to Chamberlain on May 26, "would scarcely be accredited to savages, much less to civilized and Christian people." Nevertheless, Chamberlain informed the president that "every republican meeting was interrupted by armed multitudes of democrats" and "the republican orators jeered at, interrupted, vilely insulted, and hissed down." More shoot-outs followed in Charleston on September 6, in Ellenton on September 15, and in Cainhoy on October 16. "Who commit [*sic*] these undeniable crimes against the very order and existence of society? Democrats," railed *Harper's Weekly*. "Who condone [*sic*] those crimes by silence, by incredulity, by calling them 'negro riots,' or by sneering at the bloody shirt? Democrats." In Edgefield County, Burton Stroud, a sharecropper, was told by his white employer that "by this time another year there would not be a God

10. Massachusetts senator Charles Sumner died on March 11, 1874; in this memorial tableau, Columbia lays a wreath of laurel on his casket as freed slaves kneel in sorrow and an angel, leading an angelic chorus, carries a tablet with the motto "Equal rights to all," a reference to the Civil Rights Bill that Sumner had been guiding toward passage at the time of his death.

damned radical found, and that we are determined to make away with every God damned one." When he persisted in attending "the republican speech," white Democrats tracked him to his house, shouting:

"O, Burton, look out, God damn you, we are coming for you. We have been talking about you all year and telling you to come over on the Lord's side, and you wouldn't come; and now you shan't be a radical, and you shan't be a democrat, for, God damn you, we mean to kill you and cut your head off and put it up on a stick and make a mark to shoot at, and you will vote your next ticket in hell, God damn you." And about this time they were shooting about seventy-five yards from my house. I run, and there was a ditch by the side of which there was some weeds, and I went down the hill…and they went on past me and missed me.…My wife afterward came to me, after I got out in the body of woods, and I went over to a neighbor's of mine by the name of William Collins, a colored gentleman, and my wife brought my boots and hat to me; and I asked her where was the men, and she said around there yet; and I says, "You come away from there, and come with me." Then I made for the village, and it was four weeks before I went back there any more.

When voters went to the polls on November 7, in the largest voter turnout to that point in US history, Democrats appeared to have scored their greatest victory in two decades, starting at the top with Samuel Tilden. Even Grant admitted the next morning, "Gentleman, it looks to me as if Mr. Tilden is elected."

But Grant was uncharacteristically premature in his judgment. Tilden carried New York by a whopping fifty thousand votes, but in other states, the vote count was much closer. Republican election judges in Louisiana, South Carolina, and Florida voided enough Democratic ballots to claim the electoral votes of those states for Hayes, and then to award him the election, 185 to 184. The howl of electoral robbery echoed loudly, so loudly that the editors of the *Atlantic Monthly* feared that "the national House of Representatives and Mr. Tilden have it in their power to cause an explosion in the South so terrific that the outbreak of 1860–61 will be almost forgotten." But the Democratic House and the still-Republican Senate could not agree on how to count the electoral votes, because rival totals were submitted in the three contested states, and in January 1877 Congress created a joint House-Senate Electoral Commission to determine the winner. After six weeks of bickering, Hayes was awarded all twenty contested electoral votes, just in time to be inaugurated. "I have not yet seen a single Republican who had the face to stand up and defend the act," wrote Washington lawyer James William Denver in disgust. "There will be no use in ever again holding an election." But as an olive branch to coax congressional Democrats into cooperation, Hayes signaled that he would recognize the election of Democratic governors in South Carolina and Louisiana—namely, Hampton and Francis T. Nicholls—and forbear the use of federal troops to intervene on behalf of Republican candidates and voters.

The Compromise of 1877 is often considered the end of Reconstruction—and it was, in the sense that it finally closed the door on the possibility that the federal government would play a significant role in ensuring voting rights and fair elections in the South for another eight decades. But in truth, Republican Reconstruction was as good as dead even before Hayes's inauguration. Democratic control of the House ensured that, from 1875 onward, no funding for enforcement would be forthcoming, regardless of who occupied the presidency. Federal troops in the Department of the South comprised only thirty-seven companies from five regiments, numbering no more than 1,600 officers and men, and there were only 165 federal soldiers on duty in South Carolina, and 123 in Louisiana, in 1877. In fact, Hayes did not actually have to move any troops out of the South; he merely ordered the guard company assigned to the state capitol in Columbia and the St. Louis Hotel in New Orleans returned to their quarters.

Hayes soberly believed that his administration could "be a government which guards the interests of both races carefully and equally." But it would have to operate "by the united and harmonious efforts of both races, actuated by motives of mutual sympathy and regard" which would "forever wipe out in our political affairs the color line." Where Hayes expected that upwelling of mutual sympathy and regard to come from was unclear, but no Republicans in the South expected it to come from the Democrats, who had now completed their redemption of the old Confederacy. Daniel Chamberlain surrendered the governorship he claimed to have won in South Carolina to Wade Hampton on April 10, 1877, with what could be taken as the epitaph of Reconstruction: "Today…by order of the President whom your votes alone rescued from overwhelming defeat, the Government of the United States abandons you."

Epilogue

On June 15, 1869, Patrick Sarsfield Gilmore lifted his baton before an audience of forty thousand Bostonians and gave the downbeat for ten thousand singers and one thousand instrumentalists to open the National Peace Jubilee. The five-day festival had been Gilmore's project for two years, and it gave all those performers what Boston's premier music critic, John Sullivan Dwight, hailed as a "new taste of the joy of unity of effort, a new love of co-operation, and a deeper sense of the divine significance and power of music than they ever had." Harvard's John Langdon Sibley thought it was "exceedingly exciting . . . & nearly all have gone away jubilant over what they have seen and heard." It was also depressingly premature. On the day the festival opened, congressional Reconstruction had been in operation for only two years, and four of the one-time Confederate states were still under military rule. By the time Gilmore had organized an even bigger World Peace Jubilee in June 1872—featuring a chorus of twenty thousand and orchestras and bands amounting to two thousand musicians—all ten of the reconstructed states had been readmitted to the Union, but three of them had already fallen back into the hands of Democratic "Bourbons" and "Redeemers," who were eagerly dismantling many of Reconstruction's accomplishments.

Given that dismantling, it is easy to miss what Reconstruction actually did manage to accomplish. Principally, it did, for better or worse, achieve the political reunion of the rebellious South with the rest of the nation, and did so with the basic shape of constitutional federalism reasonably intact and the chief object of the war—the elimination of legalized slavery—decided beyond challenge. The idea that states had the power to withdraw from, or break up, the American Union went down to a decisive defeat, but the importance of states within a federal republic did not. Charles Francis Adams Jr. admitted that "what is known as the doctrine of States rights...fell into much unmerited odium through its abuse during the progress of the irrepressible conflict," but "the American people still hold it in strong affection, and cling tenaciously to State lines and State authority." In time, "when the wounds of Civil War are healed...and the republic restored to its normal condition," Wisconsin Republican senator James Doolittle predicted in 1879, "the burdens of the federal government, now so crushing in their weight, will once more...rest as lightly upon our people, and its blessings will be as great to all sections as they were before that terrible convulsion" and in "our true normal condition, the burdens of the federal government will be as light as the air we breathe, though its blessings may be as vital to our well-being."

Even the strongest measures taken by the US government, during both the war and Reconstruction, were deployed less with a view toward subjugating the states to a centralized authority, and more toward nudging them back into a federal alignment. Even Lyman Trumbull's Civil Rights Bill in 1866 and the Fourteenth Amendment were largely constructed so as to prod the states to carry out the work of equal rights themselves. Trumbull assured the Senate that his bill "will have no operation in any State where the laws are equal, where all persons have the same civil rights without regard to color or race." All this was accomplished without resorting to the grimmer, retaliatory strategies of treason trials or military tribunals—and even more to the point, without triggering a renewed civil war. "Before I went South," wrote one British traveler in 1879, "I expected to find that the Southern States had been for some time in a sort of Pandaemonium in which a white man could hardly live"; instead, "to my great surprise I found exactly the contrary."

The great losers in this process were Southern blacks who, in W. E. B. Du Bois's phrase, "went free; stood a brief moment in the sun; then moved back into slavery." But even then, it was not entirely comparable to slavery; the Reconstruction amendments did recognize black citizenship and black voting rights, even if the Supreme Court acted swiftly to curtail their protection and enforcement. Black landownership not only became a reality, but increased from just 2.2 percent of Southern blacks in 1870 to 24 percent by 1910. Literacy rates rose over the same years, from 20 percent to 69 percent. These increases were not spread evenly: in the coastal plains and the mountains, 45 percent of Southern blacks owned their own land; in the Mississippi Valley and the vast "Black Belt" of northern Alabama, Georgia, and the Carolinas, only 8 percent of blacks owned their own land. In South Carolina, more than 75 percent of the lower Piedmont's twenty-four thousand tenant farmers were black, and fully half of them were sharecroppers by 1900. Even so, these circumstances, although far from ideal, were not slavery; indeed, the situation of blacks actually outstripped the condition of freed slaves and serfs in Brazil, Jamaica, and Russia.

What Southern blacks lost in wholesale amounts was political agency. The tidal return of white Democratic rule to the South by 1877 allowed the disfranchisement of black Southerners through the imposition of literacy tests, poll taxes (starting with Georgia in 1871), physical segregation, property requirements, and sheer intimidation. Disfranchisement was a surprisingly slow, incremental process. There were 9 black legislators in South Carolina in 1882, and 11 in Mississippi; as late as 1890, there were

18 blacks in the Louisiana legislature. And Republicans in Virginia and North Carolina staged brief resurgences through alliances with poor white farmers in the 1880s and 1890s, campaigning, as Thomas Settle did in North Carolina, for "no white man's party or colored man's party, but a party of principle; a party on whose banner is inscribed Liberty, union and Equality before the law; a party that proposes to elevate mankind of all races and colors." But after the turn of the century, only 1,300 blacks in Louisiana were managing to vote, and only 3,000 in Alabama and 5,000 in Texas. "Here public opinion tolerates, when it does not justify, all crimes for the maintenance of the supremacy of the Democratic party," grumbled one federal supervisor of elections for North Carolina, continuing, "Oligarchy sits enthroned by Fraud and Violence and dominates one-third of the Republic."

After the Supreme Court overturned Sumner's Civil Rights Bill in the *Civil Rights Cases* decision of 1883, Southern states began enacting statutes that banned interracial marriage, and segregated streetcars, trains, schools, dance halls, libraries, and hospitals—all of it further sanctioned by the Supreme Court's *Plessy v. Ferguson* decision in 1896. By 1920, black landownership had fallen to less than 20 percent; the 1930 census showed that of fifteen thousand locomotive engineers in the former Confederacy, only fifty were black, while 90 percent of the workers in furniture, textiles, and printing were white; by 1940, there were only eight black lawyers in Georgia and no black judges; not a single black policeman served in any of the deep South states. "The colored man is the Jean Valjean of American society," Frederick Douglass protested on the twentieth anniversary of the outbreak of the Civil War. "He has escaped from the galleys," but "the workshop denies him work, and the inn denies him shelter; the ballot-box a fair vote, and the jury-box a fair trial. He may not now be bought and sold like a beast in the market, but he is the trammeled victim of a prejudice, well calculated to repress his manly ambition, paralyze his energies, and make him a dejected and spiritless man, if not a sullen enemy to society."

The Civil War redressed the unbalancing of federalism that had been threatened by nullification and secession; but federalism thus preserved rendered the federal government unable to ensure the political stability of Reconstruction and the incorporation of the South into a national free-labor system. Instead, federalism not only tied the hands, so to speak, of Radical Republicans for political purposes, but also guaranteed the persistence of Southern peonage. "Although emancipated," John Mercer Langston warned in 1879, the freedman "has not been given practical independence of the old slave-holding class, constituting the land-proprietors and employers in the section where he lives and labors for daily support." Southern elites saw little of benefit for themselves in the free-labor ideology that they wanted to embrace, nor were there many incentives for them to do so. "Southerners used to look on the Northerners as coarse, money-getting people," complained the editors of the *Atlantic Monthly* in 1877. "Their contempt for the commercial character of the North originated . . . in the aristocratic training of the plantations, and their hatred of the liberty and equality doctrines . . . arose from the intolerance natural to all aristocracies." But it was not just the elites. Southern yeomen like Confederate apologist Leigh Robinson bundled together white supremacy and denunciations of the lure of the marketplace:

> What if the future shall say, that what the world called slavery, railed against as such, rolling up the whites of quite worldly eyes, in horror that such a thing should exist, stands forth as a patriarchal, beneficent relation, the kindest for the slave, as he came to us, not as France's "rights of man" fain would have him come; and what is now lauded to the skies, as "freedom," be exhibited, as a cruel, grasping sauve qui peut, and Devil take the hindmost, the most sordid, the most heartless of all tyranny, the one which most degradingly, and least pitifully, shoves the weakest to the wall, and keeps him there.

Free labor could even inspire a peculiarly gendered disdain, since (declared the Southern novelist Augusta Jane Evans in 1867) free labor made Northerners "effeminate, selfish, most unscrupulously grasping"; even their children were "pitiable manikins already chanting praises to the Gold Calf."

Redemption was an anti-free-labor strategy as much as it was a strategy of political exclusion. "The nigger is going to be made a serf, sure as you live," prophesied one white Alabamian to John Townsend Trowbridge in 1865. "It won't need any law for that." And not only blacks suffered from these exclusionary tactics: fully a quarter of all eligible whites in Virginia could not vote because they lacked the money to pay the state poll tax. When it was pointed out that South Carolina's "eight box law" (which required a voter to be able to read the names of candidates and the respective offices they were running for in order to place the correct ballot in one of eight ballot boxes) would disfranchise poor whites as much as blacks, the major general of the South Carolina militia merely replied, "We care not if it does." The leader of the Republican minority protested that this law had no other purpose than "keeping the middle classes and the poor whites, together with the negroes, from having anything to do with the elections," and he was not wrong. In North Carolina's Union county, not only agricultural acreage increased in the post-Reconstruction years; so too did the number of cotton plantations over one thousand acres (in Mississippi's Claiborne County, for example, the number of landholdings in the 50- to 199-acre bracket jumped from 79 to 170). Outside the principal cities, the use of cash as a medium of exchange entered only fitfully into Southern calculations. The New York Cash Store in Greenville, Alabama, advertised (despite its name) that "we will take in exchange for goods, country produce, particularly Eggs, Chickens, Bees Wax, Dry Hides, Peas, Corn Meal, and anything else that we can dispose of."

Reconstruction aspired to be a bourgeois revolution, and it expected to triumph as effortlessly as the liberal notions of progress had promised. But time sometimes does indeed go backward. In the South, the bourgeois revolution was repelled. To have achieved a different outcome would have required two ingredients—time and force—that circumstances denied Reconstruction. Wendell Phillips certainly believed that Reconstruction could hardly last less than forty years. "We have to . . . annihilate the old South, and put a new one there," and the best plan Phillips could imagine was long-term military occupation. "When England conquered the Highlands, she held them,—held them until she could educate them; and it took a generation. That is just what we have to do with the South." But Phillips was almost the only one willing to campaign for long-term military occupation. Instead, the same Romantic feudalism that had created the old Southern order reasserted its hegemony, and in another decade, the New South would link hands with Northern Progressivism in a comprehensive critique of the free-labor ideology. The bourgeoisie in this "bourgeois revolution" scenario did not flee to the aristocrats to create a "counterrevolution of property"; quite the opposite, the postwar Southern aristocrats ensured the destruction of the pure bourgeois revolution by appealing to a set of cultural and racial biases which safely defused the importance of property and sharply restricted access to it. Josephus Daniels, a North Carolina Progressive who would later serve in Woodrow Wilson's cabinet, hectored North Carolina's last black Congressman in the nineteenth century:

> It is a sad commentary upon the political conditions that have obtained in this state . . . that North Carolina should have the only nigger Congressman. . . . So far as this particular negro is personally concerned, he may be dismissed as beneath contempt. . . . The negro in office regards himself as the enemy of the white man and is anxious to have his race share in that sentiment. Therefore he becomes a menace to the peace of the Commonwealth and a danger to the safety of both races. . . . Venomous, forward, slanderous of the whites, appealing to the worst passions of his own race, he emphasizes anew the need of making an end of him and his kind.

In its passion for the organic notions of nationalism, Progressivism had scant patience for bourgeois rationalism. "Very little reflection will serve to make it clear that a community which is striving toward individual liberty as an ideal is laboring to make it easier for the strong to exploit the weak," declared North Carolina Progressive and Duke University professor William Thomas Laprade in 1916, thus intersecting racial oppression with organic progressivism. In words that could have reawakened Jefferson Davis from his tomb, Laprade said, "Nothing is more familiar to thoughtful persons than the practical antithesis between democracy and liberty," especially for a race characterized by "docility" and "untrained minds." Slavery, Laprade had written in 1911, was a system of "obligation or responsibility." While "the freedom of a slave was...seriously limited, every such limitation had a definite basis in the practices of the community [and] protected him from the cruelty of his master." As a system of reciprocity, slavery had rendered the slave "a free agent capable of acting for himself," even if the slave lacked bourgeois political rights.

Rather than a Union-approved narrative of triumphant *embougeoisment*, the overthrow of Reconstruction allowed the South to develop a series of organic nationalist myths of its own, beginning with the cult of the "Lost Cause," which argued that slavery had never been the real issue in the Civil War. "The common belief that slavery was the cause of civil war is incorrect," announced former Confederate general Richard Taylor in his 1879 memoir, *Destruction and Reconstruction*, "and Abolitionists are not justified in claiming the glory and spoils of the conflict." Instead, Southerners had been rallying to defend a unique sectional culture, and had fought a noble, heroic, and constitutionally legal war, only to be overwhelmed by Northern might. The Lost Cause became a self-sealing narrative in which heroic Southrons, "native to the soil," struggled to hold off a rapacious Yankee capitalism, and it was not unrelated to the emergence of another ideologically driven narrative of the nineteenth century, the Paris Commune. Both the legend of the Lost Cause and the legend of the Commune were expressions of a Eurocentric nostalgia for organized economies; both imagined themselves as the protectors of the oppressed, when in fact they were instruments of mayhem, leveling, and murder. Lost Causers ventured so far as to annex Abraham Lincoln, treating Lincoln's cautious political prudence as evidence that (as Kentucky journalist Henry Watterson claimed in 1902), "if Lincoln had lived there would have been no era of reconstruction, with its repressive agencies and oppressive legislation."

The Lost Cause was matched by a rival but cooperating myth: that of the "New South," which claimed, in Atlanta journalist Henry W. Grady's famous 1887 manifesto, that "there is a New South, not through protest against the Old, but because of new conditions, new adjustments and, if you please, new ideas and aspirations." New Southerners feigned an admiration for markets, striving to persuade Northern investors that the South had learned its lesson, that "we have found out that in the general summary the free Negro counts more than he did as a slave," and "that one Northern immigrant is worth fifty foreigners, and have smoothed the path to south, wiped out the place where Mason and Dixon's line used to be, and hung our latch-string out to you and yours." Adolphe J. Lafargue, who represented Avoyelles Parish in the Louisiana House of Representatives, assured all hearers in 1887 that the South was "new in brains, new in business enterprises, new in diversified industries and varied commercial pursuits, new in a reawakened agriculture, and an activity, push, thrift and a growth that is almost marvelous." This conviction allowed Woodrow Wilson to insist in 1896 that, "There is nothing to apologize for in the past of the South ... There is a great deal, however, cordially to accept in the present, and that is the consummation for which I pray and the consummation which has largely been brought about." But the assurances were hollow: the industrial renovation of the South was always an event of the future; per capita wealth in the South was less than half that of the North, and only 6 percent of the Southern labor force was involved in manufacturing by 1900. The New South was also the South of Jim Crow. And lynchings became the new way that blacks could be "counted" in the South: between 1885 and 1900, 210 lynchings took place in Alabama, 219 in Georgia, 253 in Mississippi, and 247 in Texas.

The end of Reconstruction is often spoken of in psychological terms, as a collapse of white Americans' nerve, or as a failure of Republican political will, when in cold truth Reconstruction did not fail so much as it was overthrown. Southern whites played the most obvious role in this overthrow, but they would never have succeeded without the consent of the Northern Democrats, who had never been in favor of an equitable Reconstruction, much less a bourgeois one. No such organized political opposition had arisen in Russia to obstruct Alexander II's emancipation of the serfs. Yet Democratic resistance played nearly as great—if not greater—a role in the demise of Reconstruction as Republican paralysis. From the time of Andrew Jackson, the "Democracy" had never been enthusiastic about market revolutions or bourgeois culture— those had been the property of the Whigs and then the Republicans—and they were no more enthusiastic after the war. Northern Democrats, wrote the veteran Baltimore politician John Pendleton Kennedy, "flattered the lordly ambition of the aristocratic South, courted its favor, obeyed its behests, and found a satisfactory compensation in being permitted ... to make it subservient to the selfish and sectional purpose of putting the whole Union at the foot of its slaveholding master." The Panic of 1873, the scandals of the Grant administration, and the reckless bubble of postwar finance all conspired to give new credence across the nation to the old Democratic complaints, and after the 1874 elections, Republicans would enter into more than twenty years of divided government, with neither party in control of the presidency and Congress at the same time and no hope of a rejuvenated effort to establish a national civil rights baseline along the lines of Sumner's Civil Rights Bill. The ability of the

Democratic Party to rise, phoenix-like, from the ashes of near-self-destruction in 1860 to reconquer the House of Representatives in 1874, the Senate in 1878, and the presidency in 1884, is one of the least considered aspects of Reconstruction's demise, but it is also one of the most potent.

It may be too much to have expected Republicans, even Radical Republicans, to muster the political power to resist these forces. Much had been expected from Ulysses Grant as president. But Grant, while he was long on sympathy with the freedpeople, was temperamentally inclined to react to threats to civil rights rather than designing an overarching strategy for anticipating those threats; and in any case, his inauguration as president in 1868 came after three years of Andrew Johnson in which Reconstruction's momentum lost critical pressure. Much had also been expected of Southern Unionism, but Southern Unionists turned out to be too bruised, too racist, and too willing to strike compromises with the old plantation elite. Sumner and Stevens's plan to territorialize the Confederate states might have kept any reinvigorated Southern elite from storming back into Congress and joining forces with their one-time Northern Democratic allies. However, this could scarcely have been done without the continued maintenance of a sizeble military occupation force—although given that such an occupation force would be responsible for 750,000 square miles and 9 million inhabitants, it would have required at least as many troops as were committed to pacifying the West.

As it was, the actual strength of the US Army had decreased dramatically since the last shots of the war were fired. The combined strength of the regular and volunteer forces had fallen between April 1865 and January 1866 from over 1 million men to just 90,000. Those who did remain were unenthusiastic about occupation duties. By July 1871, the army's strength stood at only 30,000, with most of those posted to the Western frontier; only 4,300 soldiers were on duty in posts in the South, and even then, mostly in major port or railroad cities. Grant used no more than 1,000 of them under the Enforcement Acts, but even that minuscule deployment did nothing to quell paranoia about "military rule," and in 1878 House Democrats would ban the use of "any part of the Army of the United States, as a posse comitatus" in most domestic cases. (The supreme irony of this gesture was that, before the war, posse comitatus was exactly what slaveholders had been demanding as a mechanism for retrieving fugitive slaves).

It is dubious whether any Congress, Republican or Democrat, would have authorized the spending needed to support an effective army of occupation, capable of suppressing Southern white insurgencies, especially with the awesome debt of the war years looming. Nor was it likely, in simple ideological terms, that Republicans could have been persuaded by anything less than outright civil war or anyone less than Abraham Lincoln to have adopted transitional military dictatorships as an acceptable way of securing republican government for any significant length of time. Military occupations strained both the patience of taxpayers and the ingrained suspicion of military rule in American minds. After the Panic of 1873 and the Democratic takeover of the House the following year, the unlikelihood shrank to the vanishing point.

If it were possible to establish a scorecard for Reconstruction, the most promising tallies would be the successful restoration of the Union as a federal Union, the legal extirpation of secession as a political tool in settling national disputes, the raising of the freed slaves to citizenship through the Fourteenth and Fifteenth Amendments, and the avoidance of mass executions and imprisonments. That Reconstruction fell short of fully implementing most of these accomplishments is its tragedy, and that tragedy can be briefly and bluntly accounted for by six factors: the sheer unpreparedness of the victorious Union to undertake something as unprecedented as a political

reconstruction of a third of its territory; the insurgent resistance
of the defeated South; the unwillingness to prolong a military
occupation to deal with that insurgency; the deaths and removal
of the Radical Republican leadership (starting with Lincoln); the
resurgence of the Northern Democrats; and, finally, the
shortsighted decisions of the federal courts.

It is also possible to say that Reconstruction might have turned out a
good deal worse than it did. Both the Civil War and Reconstruction
were remarkable for their limited durations. By the standard of civil
conflict, the American Civil War was comparatively short—the
English Civil Wars lasted seven years, and sporadic fighting
continued in Scotland and Ireland for another five; the Taiping
Rebellion lasted for fourteen; Sulla was the trigger for continual
outbreaks of civil conflict for half a century, down to Octavian and
Marc Antony. Indeed, some never seem to find any endpoint.
Reflecting on the English Civil Wars, T. S. Eliot once remarked, "The
Civil War of the seventeenth century, in which Milton is a symbolic
figure, has never been concluded.... I question whether any serious
civil war ever does end. Throughout that period English society was
so convulsed and divided that the effects are still felt."

But the American war did end, and in the span of only four years,
and Reconstruction twelve years after that, and while it is always
possible to wonder what might have happened if Reconstruction's
issues had been pressed more firmly, or its overthrow contested
more vigorously, it also has to be admitted that it might have
spiraled onward in agony and insurgency for decades, and with
every chance for a far more damaging, perhaps even genocidal,
outcome. To assume that what was eventually achieved by federal
authority in the "Second Reconstruction" in the 1960s would have
taken no more real effort from federal authority in the 1870s pays
insufficient attention to what had changed in the American
experience as a whole over those nine decades. Any proper epitaph
for Reconstruction must acknowledge that at least it managed to
avoid the fate of other post–civil war eras.

Moreover, the good fight of Reconstruction was not overthrown entirely. Post-Reconstruction Republican presidents continued to appoint attorneys general who prosecuted voting-rights violations (although the number of convictions remained ludicrously small: 20 guilty verdicts out of 282 suits during the Hayes administration, 147 out of 692 cases under presidents James Garfield and Chester Arthur), and prosecutions of the Klan won a minor victory before the Supreme Court in ex parte *Yarbrough* in 1884. For another generation after 1877, the struggles for black civil rights continued, albeit sporadically. (Union army veterans, for instance, organized the first racially integrated national society, the Grand Army of the Republic, and criticized the government's failure to give what was "promised to our colored brethren, 'forty acres and a mule.'")

Republican administrations also used the patronage they possessed for appointments of black Republicans to federal postmasterships and customs houses (especially along the long line of Southern coastal cities). As late as 1907, 244 black men and 36 black women held federal postmasterships from Republican administrations. Democrats repeatedly attempted to repeal the Enforcement Acts, only to be stymied by Republicans in the Senate and by President Hayes's vetoes, until the *Civil Rights Cases* rendered them useless by ruling that the Fourteenth Amendment gave no power to guarantee "social equality." Senate Republicans made valiant attempts to absorb equal funding for schools into the federal budget, only to have them beaten back by House Democrats. And in 1890, Massachusetts Republican Congressman Henry Cabot Lodge's elections bill (a revived Enforcement Act to provide federal oversight for mostly Southern elections) died a slow death, this time in the Senate.

But other Republicans wavered. The pressure to yield to reconciliation, to abandon black civil rights, to prevent defections by voters, and to concede talking points about race corroded the Reconstruction project. "A new era of feeling and sympathy, the ties and associations of a common ancestry and a kindred destiny" were what the *Atlantic Monthly* hoped could now be "fostered until the wounds of the past shall be cicatrized and forgotten"—by which was meant a common *white* ancestry. Benjamin Harrison, another Midwestern Republican governor and Union army veteran who was elected president in 1888, assured the all-black Harrison League of Indianapolis that Republicans were dedicated to "making all men free, and gave to you equal civil rights." But Harrison preferred, in the face of Democratic opposition (and with a view to swaying border state voters), to speak only of the "common rights of American citizenship." When a Southern delegation confronted him in 1889, Harrison hastily promised to do nothing that would place "them in positions where race instinct is sure to brew personal bitterness and social discord." He added, "I would not like to see a Negro mayor or postmaster of Indianapolis," nor would he find it "agreeable to me to practice my profession before a Colored federal judge."

Merely to call Reconstruction a failure is too simplistic. Reconstruction was overthrown, subverted, and betrayed—and then replicated, since many of the same hesitations over costs, internecine politics, and xenophobia led to dreary repetitions of these mistakes after the First World War and after the two Gulf Wars. In none of those cases would anything but lengthy and expensive occupations have sufficed to reinvent regimes that began conspiring to reverse battlefield defeat before the guns were barely cool; in none of those cases was enough of the country willing to use the force necessary to accompany liberation. "Looking back over the whole policy of reconstruction, it seems to me that the wisest thing would have been to have continued for some time the military rule," said Ulysses S. Grant:

> That was our right as a conqueror, and it was a mild penalty for the stupendous crime of treason. Military rule would have been just to all, to the negro who wanted freedom, the white man who wanted protection, the Northern man who wanted Union....The trouble about military rule in the South was that our people did not like it.

It was not in accordance with our institutions. I am clear now that it would have been better for the North to have...held the South in a territorial condition.

He was surely right, but right will not stand as right if it is realized too late. "I wonder if our white fellow-men realize the true sense or meaning of brotherhood?" demanded Susie King Taylor, a slave-born teacher and military nurse. "Was the war in vain? Has it brought freedom, in the full sense of the word, or has it not made our condition more hopeless." A century and a half later, her question still echoes horribly.

Timeline

1865

April 9	Surrender of Confederate General Robert E. Lee and his Army of Northern Virginia at Appomattox Court House
April 14	Assassination of Abraham Lincoln by John Wilkes Booth
April 15	Death of Abraham Lincoln—Andrew Johnson sworn-in as 17th President
May 10	Capture of Jefferson Davis by federal cavalry near Irwinville, Georgia
May 15	Johnson appoints Oliver Otis Howard to head Freedmen's Bureau
May 29	Johnson's amnesty proclamation
June 13-July 13	New self-reconstructed state governments established
November 22	Passage of Mississippi "black code"
December 4-July 28, 1866	Meeting of 39th Congress (1st session)
December 13	Establishment of Joint Congressional Committee on Reconstruction
December 18	Secretary of State Seward announces ratification of 13th Amendment
December 19	Passage of South Carolina "black code"

1866

January 5	Lyman Trumbull introduces bill to extend term of Freedmen's Bureau and a Civil Rights Bill
February 19	Johnson vetoes extension of Freedmen's Bureau Bill
March 27	Johnson vetoes Civil Rights Bill
April 2	Johnson proclaims ending of military hostilities
April 3	Chief Justice Chase announces Supreme Court's decision in *ex parte Milligan*
April 9	Congress passes the Civil Rights Bill over Johnson's veto
May 1-3	Memphis, Tennessee, massacre
June 13	Passage of the 14th Amendment by House of Representatives
July 30	New Orleans riot at the Mechanics Institute
August 14-16	National Union Convention meets in Philadelphia
August 27-September 15	Johnson's "Swing 'Round the Circle"
December 3-March 3, 1867	Meeting of 39th Congress (2nd session)

1867

March 2	Congress passes 1st Reconstruction Act over Johnson's veto
March 4-December 1	Meeting of 40th Congress (1st session)
March 23	Congress passes 2nd Reconstruction Act over Johnson's veto
April 1-20	Special session of 40th Congress
April 12	Chief Justice Chase delivers Supreme Court's opinion in *Texas v. White*

| July 19 | Congress passes 3rd Reconstruction Act over Johnson's veto |
| December 2–November 10, 1868 | Meeting of 40th Congress (2nd session) |

1868

March 2	Articles of impeachment of Johnson approved and managers appointed by House of Representatives
March 11	4th Reconstruction Act becomes law after Johnson fails to sign or veto
May 16	First article of impeachment fails of guilty verdict in the Senate
June 22–July 15	Congress re-admits seven Southern states under the Reconstruction Acts
July 28	Secretary of State Seward announces ratification of the 14th Amendment
August 11	Death of Thaddeus Stevens
September 19	Camilla, Georgia, massacre
September 28	Opelousas, Louisiana, massacre
November 3	Election of Ulysses S. Grant as 18th President
December 7–March 3, 1869	Meeting of 40th Congress (3rd session)

1869

March 4	Inauguration of Ulysses S. Grant as 18th President
March 4–April 10	Meeting of 41st Congress (1st session)
May 10	Leland Stanford drives ceremonial "golden spike" to open transcontinental railroad at Promontory Point, Utah Territory

June 15	Opening of National Peace Jubilee in Boston
December 6-July 15, 1870	Meeting of 41st Congress (2nd session)
December 6	Grant's first annual message to Congress

1870

January 24-July 15	Re-admission of remaining Southern states
February 25	Hiram R. Revels, first African American to be sworn-in as a U.S. Senator, takes seat once occupied by Jefferson Davis
May 31	President Grant signs the 1st Force (or Enforcement) Act
July 19	War declared between France and Prussia
October 12	death of Robert E. Lee
December 5-March 3, 1871	meeting of 41st Congress (3rd session)

1871

January 8	King Wilhelm I of Prussia proclaimed German Emperor at Versailles
February 28	Grant signs 2nd Force (or Enforcement) Act
March 4-April 20	Meeting of 42nd Congress (1st session)
March 24	Grant issues cease-and-desist proclamation to restrain political violence in South Carolina
April 20	Grant signs 3rd Force (or Enforcement) Act, also known as the Ku Klux Klan Act
June 10	U.S. Navy flotilla lands sailors and Marines in a punitive action against Korea
July 15	Death of Thomas "Tad" Lincoln, fourth child of Abraham and Mary Lincoln
October 8-10	Chicago's Great Fire
October 23	Resignation of Rufus Bullock as governor of Georgia to avoid impeachment
October 27	Arrest of William Marcy "Boss" Tweed in New York

November 10	Henry Morton Stanley "discovers" Dr. David Livingstone near Ujiji, in east Africa
December 2	Grant dismisses Amos Akerman as attorney-general
December 4–June 10, 1872	Meeting of 42nd Congress (2nd session)

1872

February 20	Opening of New York City's Metropolitan Museum of Art
May 1–3	Liberal Republican national convention meets in Cincinnati and nominates Horace Greeley for president
September 4	Crédit Mobilier scandal published by the *New York Sun*
November 5	Re-election of Ulysses Grant as President
November 29	Death of Horace Greeley
December 2–March 3, 1873	Meeting of 42nd Congress (3rd session)

1873

March 29	James Pike begins serialization of *The Prostrate State* in the *New-York Tribune*
April 13	Colfax, Louisiana, massacre
April 14	Justice Samuel Miller issues Supreme Court decision in *Slaughterhouse Cases*
May 7	Death of Chief Justice Salmon Chase
September 18	Jay Cooke & Co. closes doors of its Washington and Philadelphia offices— beginning of Panic of 1873
October 10	Assassination of Octavius V. Catto in Philadelphia
December 1–June 23, 1874	Meeting of 43rd Congress (1st session)

Timeline

1874

January 4	Inauguration of Adelbert Ames as Republican governor of Mississippi
March 11	Death of Charles Sumner
April 15-May 15	1st Impressionist exhibition opens in Paris
June 1-September 7, 1875	Congressional elections give Democrats 183-106 majority in the House of Representatives for 44th Congress
December 7-March 3, 1875	Meeting of 43rd Congress (2nd session)

1875

March 1	Grant signs Sumner's Civil Rights Bill
March 5-March 24	Meeting of 44th Congress (special session)
May 17	Running of the 1st Kentucky Derby
July 31	Death of Andrew Johnson
November 22	Death of Vice-President Henry Wilson
December 6-August 15, 1876	Meeting of 44th Congress (1st session)

1876

March 10	Alexander Graham Bell conducts first successful experiment with Telephone
March 29	Adelbert Ames agrees to resign as governor of Mississippi rather than face trumped-up charges by the Democratic state legislature
March 27	Supreme Court, with Justice Waite writing for the majority, announces decision in *U.S. v. Cruikshank*
May 10	Opening of Centennial Exhibition in Philadelphia
June 16	Republican national convention nominates Rutherford B. Hayes as its candidate for president on the seventh ballot

June 25	Battle of the Little Big Horn
June 28	Democratic national convention nominates Samuel Tilden as its candidate for president
July 8	Hamburg, South Carolina, massacre
November 7	Election day fails to produce a clear presidential winner
December 4–March 3, 1877	Meeting of 44th Congress (2nd session)

1877

January 25–26	Creation of Electoral Commission to determine winner of presidential election
March 2	Designation of Rutherford B. Hayes as 19th President
April 10	Removal of federal protection for Chamberlain government in South Carolina and surrender of state capital to Wade Hampton the next day

References

Introduction

Abraham Lincoln's comment on the idea of reconstruction are in his "First Inaugural Address" (March 4, 1861), "Proclamation of Amnesty and Reconstruction" (December 8, 1863), and "Last Public Address" (April 11, 1865), in *Collected Works of Abraham Lincoln*, ed. R.P. Basler (New Brunswick, 1953), 4:252, 7:53–4, 8:403.

Charles Sumner, "Our Domestic Relations; or, How to Treat the Rebel States," *Atlantic Monthly* 12 (October 1863), 521.

Thaddeus Stevens, *Reconstruction: Speech of the Hon. Thaddeus Stevens, Delivered in the City of Lancaster, September 7th, 1865* (Lancaster, 1865), 5, and "Reconstruction" (December 18, 1865), *Congressional Globe*, 39th Congress, 1st session, 74.

The so-called Wade-Davis Bill is the "Bill for Reconstruction," in *The Political History of the United States of America, During the Great Rebellion*, ed. Edward McPherson (Washington, 1865), 317–8.

Charles Sumner to John Bright (January 1, 1865), in *The Selected Letters of Charles Sumner*, ed. Beverly Wilson Palmer (Boston, 1990), 2:262.

Chapter One: Vengeance

Jacob Howard to Andrew Johnson (April 18, 1865), John W. Gorham to Johnson (June 3, 1865), and "Interview with Charles Halpine" (March 5, 1867), in *The Papers of Andrew Johnson: 1864–1865*, ed. LeRoy P. Graf (Knoxville, 1986), 7:580, 8:173, 12:111.

Proceedings of the Union League of Philadelphia Regarding the Assassination of Abraham Lincoln, President of the United States (Philadelphia, 1865), 19.

The beginning of Andrew Johnson's slide toward reconciliation with the defeated Confederate states is in "By the President of the United States of America—A Proclamation" (May 29, 1865), in *A Compilation of the Messages and Papers of the Presidents, 1789-1897*, ed. James D. Richardson (Washington, 1897), 6:312–314.

Thaddeus Stevens to Andrew Johnson (May 16, 1865), in *The Selected Papers of Thaddeus Stevens, Volume 2: April 1865-August 1868*, eds. B.W. Palmer & H.B. Ochoa (Pittsburgh, 1998), 5.

Sumner, "One Man Power vs. Congress—The Present Situation" (October 2, 1866), in *Charles Sumner: His Complete Works* (Boston, 1900), 14:198, 202.

"Interview with George L. Stearns" (October 3, 1865), in *The Political History of the United States of America During the Period of Reconstruction*, ed. Edward McPherson (Washington, 1875), 49.

"Laws in Relation to Freedmen," 39th Congress, 2nd session, Senate Executive Doc. No. 6 (1867), 192–199.

Hans L. Trefousse, *Thaddeus Stevens: Nineteenth-Century Egalitarian* (1997; Mechanicsburg, PA, 2001), 175.

Chapter Two: Alienation

The growing crescendo of opposition to Johnson can be seen in "Reconstruction" (December 4, 1865), "Organization of the House" (December 5, 1865), James Doolittle, "Joint Committee on Reconstruction" (December 12, 1865), Lyman Trumbull, "Civil Rights—Veto Message" (April 4, 1866), and John B. Henderson, "Reconstruction" (June 8, 1866) in *Congressional Globe*, 39th Congress, 1st session, 4–10, 26, 1755, 1760, 3034.

Johnson's riposte to the Radicals begins with his "First Annual Message" (December 4, 1865), in *Messages and Papers of the Presidents*, 6:353, 357, 360–361, 365.

Lyman Trumbull's civil rights proposals appear in his "An Act to protect all Persons in the United States in their Civil Rights, and furnish the Means of their Vindication" (April 9, 1866), in *Statutes at Large*, ed. George P. Sanger (Boston, 1868), 14:27–28.

Andrew Johnson, "Interview with a Colored Delegation respecting Suffrage" (February 7, 1866), in McPherson, *Political History* (1875), 53, 55.

"The Memphis Massacre," *Chicago Tribune* (May 9, 1865).

James Speed; A Personality (Louisville, KY, 1914), 92–93. Underscores the disenchantment of members of Johnson's cabinet with the president.

"The President on the Stump," *North American Review* 102 (April 1866), 532.

"Congress--Passage of the Civil Rights Bill in the House," *Chicago Tribune* (April 10, 1866).

"The President's Message Vetoing the Freedmen's Bureau Bill--The Bill Immediately Passed Over the Veto by Both Houses," *New York Times* (July 17, 1866).

"The Conspiracy at Washington," *Atlantic Monthly* 20 (November 1867), 634, 636–37.

The Congressional Reconstruction legislation is contained in "An Act to provide for the more efficient Government of the Rebel States" (March 2, 1867), "An Act Supplementary to an Act entitled 'An Act to provide for the more efficient Government of the Rebel States'" (March 23, 1867), "An Act Supplementary to an Act entitled 'An Act to provide for the more efficient Government of the Rebel States' (July 19, 1867) and "An Act to amend the Act passed March twenty-third, eighteen hundred and sixty-seven" (March 11, 1868), in *Statutes-at-Large, Treaties and Proclamations of the United States of America*, ed. George P. Sanger (Boston, 1868), 14:428, 15:2, 14, 41.

Chapter Three: Arrogance

On the costs of the war for the South, see Claudia D. Goldin and Frank D. Lewis, "The Economic Cost of the American Civil War: Estimates and Implications," *Journal of Economic History* 35 (June 1975), 317, and Jenny Bourne, "Double Take: Abolition and the Size of Transferred Property Rights," in *Lincoln, Congress and Emancipation*, eds. Paul Finkelman & Donald R. Kennon (Athens, OH, 2016), 228–229.

Whittier, "Snow-Bound," in *American Poetry: The Nineteenth Century, Volume One: Freneau to Whitman* (New York, 1993), 488–489.

Sidney Andrews, "Three Months Among the Reconstructionists," *Atlantic Monthly* 17 (February 1866), 238, 245.

Frederick Douglass, "Reconstruction," *Atlantic Monthly* 18 (December 1866), 762.

On the imposition of "serfdom," see "Report of an Assistant Superintendent, in Virginia" (February 26, 1866), in Walter

Lynwood Fleming, ed., *Documents Relating to Reconstruction* (Morgantown, WV, 1904), 41.

John Mercer Langston, "Citizenship and the Ballot" (October, 1865), in *Freedom and Citizenship: Selected Lectures and Addresses* (Washington, 1883), 99–100.

Examination of Cullen A. Battle (October 18, 1871), in *Testimony Taken by the Joint Select Committee to Inquire Into the Condition of Affairs in the Late Insurrectionary States* (Washington, 1872), 11:1061.

Frances Butler Leigh, *Ten Years on a Georgia Plantation Since the War* (London, 1883), 133.

"South Carolina Morals," *Atlantic Monthly* 39 (April 1877), 474.

"The Political Condition of South Carolina," *Atlantic Monthly* 39 (February 1877), 192–3.

For the Tenure of Office Act, see "An Act regulating the Tenure of certain Civil Offices" (March 2, 1867), and "An Act Making Appropriations for the Support of the Army" (March 2, 1867), in *Statutes at Large*, 14:430–32, 485–87.

"Impeachment of the President (February 22–24, 1868), *Congressional Globe*, 40th Congress, 2nd session, 1336–1369, 1382–1400.

Chapter Four: Resistance

On the nomination of Grant, see *Official Proceedings of the National Republican Conventions of 1868, 1872, 1876 and 1880* (Minneapolis, 1903), 28, 78.

"South Carolina—The Reconstruction Convention," *New York Times* (January 21, 1868).

Tourgee, "Speech on Elective Franchise" (February 22, 1868), in *Undaunted Radical: The Selected Writings and Speeches of Albion W. Tourgée*, eds. Mark Elliott & J.D. Smith (Baton Rouge, 2010), 39.

Albert T. Morgan, *Yazoo: Or, On the Picket Line of Freedom in the South* (Washington, 1884), 25.

"The Mission of the War—A Lecture by Frederick Douglass," *New-York Tribune* (January 14, 1864).

"The Political Condition of South Carolina," *Atlantic Monthly* 39 (February 1877), 186.

Examination of Leander Bigger (July 15, 1871), in *Testimony Taken by the Joint Select Committee to Inquiry into the Condition of Affairs in the Late Insurrectionary States* (Washington, 1872), 1:276.

Depositions of Spencer Griffith, Charles E. Robert, S.C. Mercer and
      H.H. Aynett (August 27 and 29, 1868), in *Report of Evidence Taken
      Before the Military Committee: In Relation to Outrages Committed
      by the Ku Klux Klan in Middle and Western Tennessee* (Nashville,
      1868), 55–56, 59.
T. Thomas Fortune, *After War Times: An African American Childhood
      in Reconstruction-Era Florida*, ed. D.R. Weinfeld (Tuscaloosa,
      2014), 17.

Chapter Five: Distraction

Ulysses S. Grant to Joseph Hawley (May 29, 1868) and to
      Edward R.S. Canby (June 26, 1868), in *The Papers of Ulysses
      Grant*, ed. John Y. Simon (Carbondale, IL, 1991), 18:264, 296;
      "Inaugural Address," in *Messages and Papers of the Presidents*,
      7:6–8.
On Adolph "Bovie," see William Livingstone, *Livingstone's History of
      the Republican Party* (Detroit: Wm. Livingstone, 1900), 1:244.
"His mind seemed torpid" appears in *The Education of Henry Adams:
      An Autobiography* (Boston: Houghton Mifflin, 1918), 263–264.
Grant, "First Annual Message" (December 6, 1869), in *Messages and
      Papers of the Presidents*, 7:28–29.
On the re-admission of Southern states, see "Right of Representation"
      (January 25, 1870), in *Congressional Globe*, 41st Congress, 2nd
      session, 720, 759; "An Act to admit the State of Virginia to
      Representation in the Congress of the United States" (January 26,
      1870), in *Statutes at Large*, 16:62–63.
On landownership patterns, see Jonathan Weiner, "Planter Persistence
      and Social Change: Alabama, 1850-1870," *Journal of
      Interdisciplinary History* 7 (Autumn 1976), 237–38, 241, 257.
The Force Acts are itemized as "An Act to enforce the Right of Citizens
      of the United States to Vote in the Several States of this Union, and
      for other Purposes" (May 31, 1870), "An Act to enforce the Rights
      of Citizens of the United States to Vote in the Several States of this
      Union" (February 28, 1871), and "An Act to enforce the Provisions
      of the Fourteenth Amendment to the Constitution of the United
      States" (April 20, 1871) in *Statutes-at-Large*, 16:140–46, 433–40
      and 17:13–15.
Testimony of Elias Hill (July 25, 1871), in *Testimony Taken by the
      Joint Select Committee to Inquire into The Condition of Affairs in
      the Late Insurrectionary States* (Washington, 1872), 3:1411.

Edward Townsend to Alfred Terry (September 11, 1871) and Grant to
Akerman (December 12, 1871), in *Papers of Ulysses S. Grant*,
22:180, 288.

George Ward Nichols, "The Indian: What Should We Do With Him,"
Harper's New Monthly Magazine 40 (April 1870), 733.

Concerning Reconstruction in Mormon Utah, see "The Mormons,"
New York Herald (March 25, 1872), John Hay, "The Mormon
Prophet's Tragedy," *Atlantic Monthly* 24 (December1869), 679, and
"Polygamy in Utah" (March 23, 1870), *Congressional Globe*, 41st
Congress, 2nd session, 2181.

On the Liberal Republicans, see "The Failure of the Confidence Game,"
Harper's Weekly (November 9, 1872).

Chapter Six: Law

On the reconstruction of the federal judiciary after the Civil War, see
William M. Wiecek, "The Reconstruction of Federal Judicial
Power, 1863-1875," *American Journal of Legal History* 13 (October
1969), 333.

For the role of Salmon Chase as chief justice, see Chase to J.M. Reid
(January 29, 1865) to Lincoln (April 11, 1865), to Henry Hilliard
(April 27, 1868) and to J.W. Schuckers (September 24, 1866), in
Jacob W. Schuckers, *The Life and Public Services of Salmon
Portland Chase* (New York, 1874), 514–5, 520, 528, 541; see also
Chase to William S. Rosecrans (August 16, 1869), in *The
Salmon P. Chase Papers: Correspondence, 1865–1873*, ed. John
Niven (Kent, OH, 1998), 5:314.

Cummings v. The State of Missouri, in *Cases Argued and Adjudged in
the Supreme Court of the United States, December Term, 1866*, ed.
J.W. Wall (Washington, 1870), 4:285.

On the 15th Amendment, see "Suffrage" (January 11 and 29, 1869), in
Congressional Globe, 40th Congress, 3rd session, 285, 723, and
"The Suffrage Amendments in Congress," *New York Times*
(February 15, 1869).

Texas v. White et al, in *Cases Argued and Adjudged in the Supreme
Court of the United States, December Term 1868*, 7:703.

Slaughter-House Cases (The Butchers' Benevolent Association of New
Orleans v. The Crescent City Live Stock Landing and Slaughter-
House Company), in *Reports of Cases Argued and Decided in the
Supreme Court of the United States in the December Term, 1872*,

and *October Term, 1873*, ed. Stephen K. Williams (Newark, NY, 1884), 21:408.

United States v. William J. Cruikshank et al (1876), in *Reports of Cases Argued and Decided in the Supreme Court of the United States in the October Terms, 1874, 1875, 1876*, ed.
Stephen K. Williams (Newark, NY, 1885), 23:588–97.

Chapter Seven: Dissension

"The King of Frauds—How the Credit Mobilier Bought Its Way Through Congress" and "The Credit Mobilier and the Bribery of Members of Congress," *New York Sun* (September 4 and 10, 1872).

James S. Pike, *The Prostrate State: South Carolina Under Negro Government* (New York, 1874), 12, 14.

"Wall-St. Panic-Stricken," *New-York Tribune* (September 19, 1873).

Daniel R. Biddle & Murray Dubin, *Tasting Freedom: Octavius Catto and the Battle for Equality in Civil War America* (Philadelphia, 2010), 428–429.

Tilton, "One Blood of All Nations" (February 27, 1864), in *Sanctum Sanctorum; or, Proof-Sheets from an Editor's Table* (New York, 1870).

Dennett, "The South As It Is," *The Nation* (January 4, 1866). See also Current, *Those Terrible Carpetbaggers*, 369–70 and Ruth Currie McDaniel, *Carpetbagger of Conscience: A Biography of John Emory Bryant* (Athens, GA, 1987),148, 176, 178.

"The Week," *The Nation* (September 23, 1875).

"State of Georgia" (March 15, 1870), in *Congressional Globe*, 41st Congress, 2nd session, 1956.

On dissension within Reconstruction's ranks, see Mrs. A.M. French, *Slavery in South Carolina and the Ex-Slaves; or, The Port Royal Mission* (New York, 1862), 136, 138, and Turner, in Currie-McDaniel, *Carpetbagger of Conscience*, 95, and Jones, *A Dreadful Deceit*, 177–178.

Julia Crofts to Douglass (April 13, 1863), in Douglas R. Egerton, *Thunder at the Gates: The Black Civil War Regiments that Redeemed America* (New York, 2016), 77.

Sumner's Civil Rights Bill is contained in "An Act to protect all citizens in their civil and legal rights" (March 1, 1875), *Statutes-at-Large*, 18:335–337.

Jerry L. West, *The Bloody South Carolina Election of 1876: Wade Hampton III, the Red Shirt Campaign for Governor and the End of Reconstruction* (Jefferson, NC, 2011), 69–72.

Chamberlain's farewell is part of "To the Republicans of South
Carolina" (April 10, 1877), in Walter Allen, *Governor Chamberlain's
Administration in South Carolina: A Chapter of Reconstruction in
the Southern States* (New York, 1888), 481.

Epilogue

C.F. Adams, "The Government and the Railroad Corporations," *North
American Review* 112 (January 1871), 35, 51, and J.R. Doolittle,
"Law Address of Ex-Senator James R. Doolittle, Delivered before
the Union College of Law at Chicago, June 6th, 1879," *Journal of the
Illinois State Historical Society* 19 (April-July 1926), 84.

Frederick Douglass, "National Colored Convention" (April 15, 1872), in
*The American Annual Cyclopedia and Register of Important
Events of the Year 1872* (New York, 1873), 775.

John Mercer Langston, "The Exodus" (1879), in *Freedom and
Citizenship: Selected Lectures and Addresses* (Washington, 1883), 238.

W.T. Laprade, "A New Epoch," in *Proceedings of the Seventeenth
Annual Session of the State Library and Historical Association of
North Carolina, Raleigh, December 5-6, 1916* (Raleigh, 1917),
51–53, 55, and "Some Problems in Writing the History of American
Slavery," *South Atlantic Quarterly* 10 (April 1911), 138–39.

On the formulation of a "Lost Cause" and "New South" mythology, see
Richard Taylor, *Destruction and Reconstruction: Personal
Experiences of the Late War* (London, 1879), 2, and
Henry W. Grady, "The New South" (December 22, 1886), in Joel
Chandler Harris, *Henry W. Grady: His Life, Writings, and
Speeches* (New York, 1890), 15–16.

"Over 3,000 Lynchings in Twenty Years," *Chicago Tribune* (September
1, 1901).

On Grant's reflection on military occupation, see John Russell Young,
Around the World with General Grant (New York, 1879), 2:362–63

Susie King Taylor, *Reminiscences of My Life in Camp with the 33[d]
United States Colored Troops* (Boston, 1902), 61.

Further reading

Introduction

William Archibald Dunning gave birth to the school of Reconstruction interpretation which pictured white Southerners, not the freed slaves, as the victims of vengeful Northerners. Dunning's view, in *Reconstruction: Political & Economic, 1865–1877* (1905), was challenged by W.E.B. DuBois in *Black Reconstruction in America*, (1935), by Kenneth M. Stampp in *The Era of Reconstruction, 1865–1877* (1967), and Eric Foner in *Reconstruction: America's Unfinished Revolution, 1863–1877* (1988), all of which were shaped in varying degrees by Marxist influences. Barrington Moore, *Social Origins of Dictatorship and Democracy: Lord and Peasant in the Making of the Modern World* (1967) proposed interpreting Reconstruction as a bourgeois revolution.

Lincoln's ideas on Reconstruction are treated in Louis P. Masur, *Lincoln's Last Speech: Wartime Reconstruction and the Crisis of Reunion* (2015) and William C. Harris, *With Charity for All: Lincoln and the Restoration of the Union* (1997). A more expansive view of Reconstruction is contained in Heather Cox Richardson's *The Death of Reconstruction: Race, Labor, and Politics in the Post-Civil War North, 1865–1901* (2001) and *West from Appomattox: The Reconstruction of America after the Civil War* (2008). Douglas Egerton's *The Wars of Reconstruction: The Brief, Violent History of America's Most Progressive Era* (2014) and Mark Wahlgren Summers' *The Ordeal of the Reunion: A New History of Reconstruction* (2014) illuminate the political upheavals of Reconstruction.

Four important anthologies bring together an array of important primary sources on Reconstruction: Edward McPherson, *The Political History of the United States of America During the Period of Reconstruction* (1875), Walter L. Fleming's *Documentary History of Reconstruction: Political, Military, Social, Religious, Educational, and Industrial* (2 vols.,1906), John David Smith's *We Ask Only for Even-Handed Justice: Black Voices from Reconstruction, 1865–1877* (2014), and Brooks Simpson's *Reconstruction: Voices from America's First Great Struggle for Racial Equality*, in the Library of America series (2018).

Chapter One: Vengeance

The most revealing memoirs of individuals at the center of the events in Washington which launched Reconstruction are *John Sherman's Recollections of Forty Years in the House, Senate and Cabinet* (1895), George Boutwell's *Reminiscences of Sixty Years in Public Affairs* (1902); James G. Blaine's *Twenty Years of Congress: from Lincoln to Garfield* (1886), George W. Julian's *Political Recollections, 1840–1872* (1884), the *Diary of Gideon Welles*, ed. E.T. Welles (3 vols., Boston, 1911), and Chauncey M. Depew's *My Memories of Eighty Years* (1922).

Among the first-hand views of the South immediately after the end of the war, Sidney Andrews' *The South Since the War: As Shown by Fourteen Weeks of Travel and Observation in Georgia and the Carolinas* (Boston, 1866), John Townsend Trowbridge's *The South: A Tour of Its Battlefields and Ruined Cities* (1867), and Whitelaw Reid's *After the War: A Southern Tour, May 1, 1865, to May 1, 1866* (1866) are the most comprehensive.

The principal biographers of Andrew Johnson are Eric L. McKitrick, in *Andrew Johnson and Reconstruction* (1960, 1988) and Hans L. Trefousse, in *Andrew Johnson: A Biography* (1989). Gregory Downs, *After Appomattox: Military Occupation and the Ends of War* (2015), offers the fullest survey of Union military occupation of the South.

Chapter Two: Alienation

The Freedmen's Bureau still begs for a comprehensive history, but John and LaWanda Cox's "General O.O. Howard and the

'Misrepresented Bureau,'" *Journal of Southern History* 19 (November 1953) remains a fine introduction. Paul H. Bergeron, *Andrew Johnson and Reconstruction* (2011), is an important guide to the steady deterioration of Johnson's authority in 1866–67. On the horrendous race riots in New Orleans and Memphis, which played a significant role in undercutting that authority, see Hannah Rosen, *Terror in the Heart of Freedom: Citizenship, Sexual Violence, and the Meaning of Race in the Postemancipation South* (2009), James G. Hollandsworth, *An Absolute Massacre: The New Orleans Race Riot of July 30, 1866* (2001), and Stephen V. Ash, *A Massacre in Memphis: The Race Riot That Shook the Nation One Year After the Civil War* (2013). Joseph G. Dawson's *Army Generals and Reconstruction: Louisiana, 1862–1877* (1982) is a model in describing the difficulties in implementing Congressional Reconstruction. Mark Wahlgren Summers's *A Dangerous Stir: Fear, Paranoia, and the Making of Reconstruction* (2009) untangles the rumored plan of Andrew Johnson to stage a military coup of his own against Congress.

Chapter Three: Arrogance

For the meaning of free labor, see Eric Foner, *Free Soil, Free Labor, Free Men: The Ideology of the Republican Party Before the Civil War* (1970), Michael S. Green, *Freedom, Union, and Power: Lincoln and His Party during the Civil War* (2004), and Heather Cox Richardson, *The Death of Reconstruction*. The struggles of the freed slaves to establish economic independence for themselves in Georgia and North Carolina are handled in Paul A. Cimbala, *Under the Guardianship of the Nation: The Freedmen's Bureau and the Reconstruction of Georgia, 1865–1870* (1997) and Patricia C. Click, *Time Full of Trial: The Roanoke Island Freedmen's Colony, 1862–1867* (2001). The standard works on the impeachment of Andrew Johnson are David O. Stewart, *Impeached: The Trial of President Johnson and the Fight for Lincoln's Legacy* (2009) and Michael Les Benedict's classic, *The Impeachment and Trial of Andrew Johnson* (1973). James Ashley's lead role in the impeachment itself can be followed in Robert F. Horowitz, *The Great Impeacher: A Political Biography of James M. Ashley* (1979).

Chapter Four: Resistance

Few groups in American history have been more utterly misrepresented than the 'carpetbaggers,' whom the Dunning school routinely represented as Northern harpies who, in league with ignorant blacks and opportunistic Southern 'scalawags,' appeared at the end of the war to rip out profit from the body of a prostrate South. Revision of this farcical picture begins with Richard M. Current's *Those Terrible Carpetbaggers: A Reinterpretation* (1988), David S. Cecelski, *The Fire of Freedom: Abraham Galloway and the Slaves' Civil War* (2012), Canter Brown, *Florida's Black Public Officials, 1867–1924* (1998), Mark Elliott, *Color-Blind Justice: Albion Tourgée and the Quest for Racial Equality from the Civil War to Plessy v. Ferguson* (2006), Nancy Koester, *Harriet Beecher Stowe: A Spiritual Life* (2014), and Ruth Currie-McDaniel, *Carpetbagger of Conscience: A Biography of John Emory Bryant* (1987). The 'scalawags' in particular have benefitted from sympathetic treatment through James Alex Baggett, *The Scalawags: Southern Dissenters in the Civil War and Reconstruction* (2003), Sarah Woolfolk Wiggins, *The Scalawag In Alabama Politics, 1865–1881* (1977), and Richard L. Hume and Jerry B. Gough, *Blacks, Carpetbaggers, and Scalawags: The Constitutional Conventions of Radical Reconstruction* (2008).

The recreation of a resistant Southern sectional identity, continuous with the Confederacy, has been ably analyzed in Anne Sarah Rubin in *A Shattered Nation: The Rise and Fall of the Confederacy, 1861–1868* (2005). The terrorist insurgency mounted by the Ku Klux Klan and other white supremacist militias can be followed in Wyn Craig Wade, *The Fiery Cross: The Ku Klux Klan in America* (1998), Stephen Budiansky, *The Bloody Shirt: Terror After Appomattox* (2006), Edward John Harcourt, "Who Were the Pale Faces? New Perspectives on the Tennessee Ku Klux Klan," *Civil War History* 51 (March 2005), Lee W. Formwalt, "The Camilla Massacre of 1868: Racial Violence as Political Propaganda," *George Historical Quarterly*, 71 (Fall 1987), James G. Dauphine, "The Knights of the White Camellia and the Election of 1868: Louisiana's White Terrorists," *Louisiana History* 30 (Spring 1989), and Carolyn E. DeLatte, "The St. Landry Riot: A Forgotten Incident of Reconstruction Violence," *Louisiana History* 17 (Winter 1976), 47–48.

Chapter Five: Distraction

On the economic conditions which prevailed in the South during Reconstruction and after, the primary work is Edward L. Ayres, *The Promise of the New South: Life After Reconstruction* (1992). But there are also a number of useful studies of specific components of that economy, starting with William J. Cooper, "The Cotton Crisis in the Antebellum South: Another Look," *Agricultural History* 49 (April 1975) and Robert Tracy McKenzie, "Freedmen and the Soil in the Upper South: The Reorganization of Tennessee Agriculture, 1865-1880," *Journal of Southern History* 59 (February 1993).

The reputation of Ulysses Grant as a president has suffered nearly as much obloquy as the 'carpetbaggers,' and with as little justification. Substantial work in retrieving Grant's reputation has been done by Brooks D. Simpson in *Let Us Have Peace: Ulysses S. Grant and the Politics of War and Reconstruction, 1861–1868* (1991) and *The Reconstruction Presidents* (1998), H.W. Brands, *The Man Who Saved the Union: Ulysses Grant in War and Peace* (2012), Charles W. Calhoun, *The Presidency of Ulysses S. Grant* (2017), and Ron Chernow, *Grant* (2018). On Grant's suppression of the Ku Klux Klan in South Carolina, see Lou Falkner Williams, "The South Carolina Ku Klux Klan Trials and Enforcement of Federal Rights, 1871-1872," *Civil War History* 39 (March 1993), and Jerry Lee West, *The Reconstruction Ku Klux Klan in York County, South Carolina, 1865-1877* (Jefferson, NC: McFarland, 2002).

On the unhappy and short-lived Liberal Republican movement, see Andrew L. Slap, *The Doom of Reconstruction: The Liberal Republicans in the Civil War Era* (2006), and Hans L. Trefousse, *Carl Schurz: A Biography* (1982).

Chapter Six: Law

The federal courts were consigned to a curiously diminished role during the Civil War, as explained by Mark E. Neely, *Lincoln and the Triumph of the Nation: Constitutional Conflict in the American Civil War* (2011) and Jonathan W. White, "The Strangely Insignificant Role of the U.S. Supreme Court during the Civil War," *Journal of the Civil War Era* 3 (June 2013). The determination of the jurists to re-capture their lost standing can be seen in

Joseph G. Gambone, "Ex Parte Milligan: The Restoration of Judicial Prestige," *Civil War History* 16 (September 1970).

The dominant figures of the Reconstruction Supreme Court begin with Salmon Chase, as Chief Justice. Chase has benefited from several comprehensive biographies and studies, by Michael Les Benedict in "Salmon P. Chase and Constitutional Politics," *Preserving the Constitution: Essays on Politics and the Constitution in the Reconstruction Era* (2006), Jacob W. Schuckers, *The Life and Public Services of Salmon Portland Chase* (1874), Frederick J. Blue, *Salmon P. Chase: A Life in Politics* (1987) and John Niven, *Salmon P. Chase: A Biography* (1995). Chase's papers (principally correspondence) have also been collected by Niven in five volumes, covering 1829 to 1873, and published by Kent State University Press. Michael A. Ross's *Justice of Shattered Dreams: Samuel Freeman Miller and the Supreme Court during the Civil War Era* (2003) and Willard L. King's *Lincoln's Manager: David Davis* (1960) capture the lives of two other influential justices of the Court, but Joseph P. Bradley, who played an outsize role in the decisions in *Slaughterhouse Cases* and *U.S. v. Cruikshank* still goes a-begging for a biographer. Those cases have been dramatically handled in Ronald M. Labbé and Jonathan Lurie, *The Slaughterhouse Cases: Regulation, Reconstruction, and the Fourteenth Amendment* (2003), Charles Lane, *The Day Freedom Died: The Colfax Massacre, the Supreme Court, and the Betrayal of Reconstruction* (2008), and LeeAnna Keith, *The Colfax Massacre: The Untold Story of Black Power, White Terror, and the Death of Reconstruction* (2008).

The 14th and 15th Amendments have found skillful examiners in John Mabry Mathews, *Legislative and Judicial History of the Fifteenth Amendment* (1909), Pamela Brandwein, *Rethinking the Judicial Settlement of Reconstruction* (2011), Kurt T. Lash, *The Fourteenth Amendment and the Privileges and Immunities of American Citizenship* (2014), Gerard Magliocca, *American Founding Son: John Bingham and the Invention of the Fourteenth Amendment* (2013) and Michael Les Benedict, "At Every Fireside: Constitutional Politics in the Era of Reconstruction," in *Constitutionalism in the Approach and Aftermath of the Civil War*, eds. Paul D. Moreno & Johnathan O'Neill ((2013).

Chapter Seven: Dissension

The final stages of Reconstruction's overthrow, especially in Louisiana and South Carolina after the Hayes-Tilden presidential contest, have been told well and often in

A.J. Langguth, *After Lincoln: How the North Won the Civil War and Lost the Peace* (2014), Stetson Kennedy, *After Appomattox: How the South Won the War* (1995), Nicholas Lemann, *Redemption: The Last Battle of the Civil War* (2006), and Michael Perman, *The Road to Redemption: Southern Politics, 1869–1879* (1984). Some of the wounds were self-inflicted, among both black and white Republicans, and these are described in Michael W. Fitzgerald, *Urban Emancipation: Popular Politics in Reconstruction Mobile, 1860–1890* (2002), Philip B. Lyons, *Statesmanship and Reconstruction: Moderate versus Radical Republicans on Restoring the Union after the Civil War* (2014) and Jacqueline Jones, *A Dreadful Deceit: The Myth of Race from the Colonial Era to Obama's America* (2013). The crises in Louisiana and South Carolina are chronicled in Jerry L. West, *The Bloody South Carolina Election of 1876: Wade Hampton III, the Red Shirt Campaign for Governor and the End of Reconstruction* (2011) and William Gillette, *Retreat from Reconstruction, 1869–1879* (1979). Paul Leland Haworth laid out a detailed account of the contested 1876 presidential election in *The Hayes-Tilden Disputed Presidential Election of 1876* (1906), to be followed by Roy Morris in *Fraud Of The Century: Rutherford B. Hayes, Samuel Tilden And The Stolen Election Of 1876* (2004) and Michael F. Holt in *By One Vote: The Disputed Presidential Election of 1876* (2008).

Epilogue

Might-have-beens cluster thickly around Reconstruction, especially concerning economic issues. Land re-distribution, as described by Claude F. Oubre, *Forty Acres and a Mule: The Freedmen's Bureau and Black Land Ownership* (1978), might have been one solution; more aggressive federal defence of voting rights might have been another, as can be seen from Michael Perman, *Struggle for Mastery: Disfranchisement in the South, 1888–1908* (2001).

Peter Kolchin has provided the important reminder, though, that not everything in Reconstruction was a failure, especially when compared to other 19th-century emancipations, which he does in

"Comparative Perspectives on Emancipation in the U.S. South: Reconstruction, Radicalism and Russia," *Journal of the Civil War Era* 2 (June 2012) and "Thoughts on Emancipation in Comparative Perspective: Russia and the United States South," *Slavery and Abolition* 11 (December 1990).

On the formulation of Southern regional myths after Reconstruction, the basic texts have long been Paul Gaston, *The New South Creed: A Study in Southern Mythmaking* (1973) and C. Vann Woodward, *The Burden of Southern History* (1968).

Index

A

Adams, Charles Francis, 86
Adams, Charles Francis, Jr., 121
Adams, Henry, 73
African Americans, 8, 10, 12, 13, 14, 15, 16 17, 18, 27, 31, 33, 36, 37, 43, 45–51, 52, 53, 58, 60, 61, 62–68, 70, 74, 76–82, 84, 86, 91, 94, 96, 99, 100, 104–07, 109, 112–115, 122–23, 125–26, 129, 134–137
Akerman, Amos Tappan (attorney general), 81–2
Alabama, 19, 23, 26, 27, 32, 47, 50, 52, 53, 58, 59, 61, 63, 68, 69, 77, 79, 80, 91, 106, 110, 122, 125, 129
Alcorn, James Lusk, 70, 74, 108–09
Allen, James S., 10
Allston, Elizabeth, 49
Alston, James, 50
American Freedman's Union Commission, 51
American Missionary Association, 51, 78, 111
Ames, Adelbert, 70, 74, 108, 111
Antoine, Caesar Carpentier, 112
Appomattox Court House, Virginia, 18

Arizona, 82
Arkansas, 2, 6, 32, 52, 59, 60, 64, 65, 70, 72, 80, 106, 110
Arthur, Chester Alan (twenty-first president), 133
Ashley, James Mitchell, 56, 71
Atlantic Monthly, 47, 67, 117, 124, 134

B

Babcock, Orville, 102
Barron v. Baltimore (1833), 96
Barton, Clara, 36
Bates, George, 85
Battle, Cullen Andrews, 26, 50
Baxter, Elisha, 110
Beckwith, James Roswell, 99
Belgium, 3
Belknap, William Worth (secretary of war), 102
Bell, Alexander Graham, 102
Belmont, August, 2
Berry, Lawrence S., 111
Bingham, John Armor, 71. 95
"black codes," 27, 48, 94
Blaine, James Gillespie, 80
Booth, John Wilkes, 16, 18, 19, 20
Boston, Massachusetts, 102, 120
"Bourbons," 120

W

Wade, Benjamin Franklin, 4–5, 28–9, 75, 106
  and Wade-Davis Reconstruction plan, 4–5
Waite, Morrison Remick (chief justice), 90, 98, 99, 100
Walker, Gilbert, 70
Warmoth, Henry Clay, 63, 70, 98, 110
Washburne, Elihu, 72, 73
Watterson, Henry, 128
Welles, Gideon (secretary of the navy), 28, 33, 40, 73
Wells, James Madison, 37
West, George Benjamin, 48
Whiskey Rebellion, 3
White, Richard, 112
White Leagues, 66, 80

White Liners, 109
Whitman, Walt, 12, 43
Whittier, John Greenleaf, 46
Wilkinson, Morton, 29, 82
Williams, George Henry (attorney general), 82
Wilson, Henry (eighteenth vice president), 75, 114
Wilson, Reuban, 25
Wilson, Thomas Woodrow (28th president), 126, 128
Winthrop, Robert Charles, 39
Wisconsin, 31, 36, 121
Wood, Fernando, 38
Woodruff, Josephus, 76

Y

Young, Brigham, 84–5